BEYOND THE SOILED CURTAIN

PROJECT RESCUE'S FIGHT FOR THE VICTIMS OF THE SEX SLAVE INDUSTRY

DAVID & BETH GRANT

Beyond the Soiled Curtain
Project Rescue's Fight for the Victims
of the Sex-Slave Industry
By David and Beth Grant

Ninth Printing

Printed in the United States of America
ISBN: 1-880689-19-7
Copyright 2007, 2009, David and Beth Grant and
Onward Books, Inc.

Cover design by KeyArt
Cover photography by David Dobson

Unless otherwise indicated, all Scripture references
are from the *Holy Bible: New International Version*,
copyright 1984, Zondervan Bible Publishers. Scripture
quotations marked *KJV* are from the *King James
Version* of the Bible.

Many of the names used in this book have been
changed. Some circumstances and identities
have been altered, but not in such a way as to
distort the truth of the story or portrayal of the
characters.

DEDICATION

To Dr. Charles Greenaway,
a mentor in missions, who challenged us to go
with our strengths, vision and passion.

To Dr. Mark Buntain,
a mentor in compassion, who opened our hearts
to the broken heart of Jesus for India's poor.

To the Reverend Curtis Grant,
a father and a mentor in ministry, who inspired
his son to give generously to God and missions
from the time he was born.

To our daughters, Rebecca and Jennifer,
who have generously shared their hearts, faith and
tears in believing with us that God could take the
most broken of India's daughters and transform
them into courageous women of God.

CONTENTS

ENDORSEMENTS

It is an honor for me to recommend the ministry of Project Rescue in India. David and Beth Grant and Brother K.K. Devaraj are very dear friends and colleagues with us in challenging this evil darkness on our continent. By God's grace, the lives of thousands of women and children have been touched for eternity.

> Dr. D. Mohan
> General Superintendent
> All-India Assemblies of God

When a task needs to be done God often lays it upon the hearts of His servants. So is the ministry of David and Beth Grant and Project Rescue, a ministry to women and children enslaved in prostitution in Bombay, India. We commend them for obeying the voice of the Lord in reaching out to these forgotten people.

> Dr. Thomas E. Trask
> Former General Superintendent
> U.S. Assemblies of God

As Project Rescue celebrates its 10-year mark of compassionate ministry to women and children enslaved in prostitution, the Assemblies of God honors the ministry's mark on our movement. God has used this pioneering effort to invade one of the greatest evils of our day. Jesus began His ministry by declaring that He had come to set the captives free. Project Rescue is a vital ministry that fulfills Jesus' desire to "set at liberty those who are oppressed." May Project Rescue's impact in days to come be far greater than ever because of the faithful support of those who share the heart of Jesus for the victims of man's inhumanity to women and children.

Dr. George O. Wood
General Superintendent
U.S. Assemblies of God

Project Rescue, under the leadership of David and Beth Grant, has pioneered a path of rescue for women and girls trapped in the global sex industry. This is one of the few organizations bringing life-changing aftercare to women and children who are facing the horrors of sexual exploitation from trafficking. Through a powerful proclamation of faith in Jesus Christ and His power to heal, Project Rescue is bringing hope in Eurasia to those who otherwise have no hope.

Jerry Parsley
Former Eurasia Regional Director
Assemblies of God World Missions

Project Rescue is bringing hope, and changing the lives of hurting women and their precious children in countries across Southern Asia. The passion of David and Beth Grant is seen and felt as they have reached out with tender and loving compassion to thousands who have been degraded and corrupted. They have opened the door to restoration and redemption through Jesus Christ. I am extremely pleased to partner with this marvelous ministry and their staff, who make extreme sacrifices to touch lives with the heart of God.

David Burdine
Former Chairman of the Board
Bethesda Outreach Ministries

Project Rescue was born from a passion of true care and concern for the lost and hurting. Being aware of this compassionate ministry from its beginning, I fully endorse the level of quality and execution of a program that is affecting the destinies of those caught in one of the darkest atrocities of our day.

David Perkin
Chairman of the Board
Bethesda Ministries/Mission of Mercy

ACKNOWLEDGMENTS

To our courageous Project Rescue colleagues who have dared to confront one of our world's darkest evils to bring hope and healing in Jesus' name.

To Alton Garrison, Rod Loy and First Assembly of God, North Little Rock, Arkansas, who gave the first generous gift to purchase land for the first Home of Hope in Bombay.

To Judy Rachels and the women of Southern California who embraced Project Rescue as their own and raised the funding to help rescue hundreds of women and children.

To Jerry Parsley, our Eurasia Regional Director for AG World Missions, who believed in this vision and gave us his blessing to pursue it in faith.

STATISTICS *

* Following statistics are the most conservative estimates available.

- 2 million children are exploited in the global commercial sex trade each year.

- Of the millions trafficked across international borders every year, 80 percent are women and girls and 50 percent are minors.

- The International Labor Organization estimates that there are 12.3 million people in modern day slavery, including sexual exploitation, at any given time. Other estimates range from 4 million to 27 million.

- Human trafficking has exploded into a multi-billion dollar global industry with sexual trafficking constituting a major part. Profits from sex trafficking are estimated to be as high as $19 billion annually.[1]

- A 2004 UNICEF report estimated that India supplied 50% of the children worldwide entering into the sex trade.[2]

- Each year, 12,000 Nepalese children, mostly girls, are trafficked within Nepal or to brothels in India and other countries for commercial sexual exploitation.[3]

- 2.3 million women and girls are prostituted and/or working as madams in India.[4]

- Moldova is a major source of women and girls trafficked for the purpose of sexual exploitation. It is estimated that 1% of Moldovans working abroad are victims of trafficking.[1]

- As many as 17,500 people are trafficked into the United States every year for the purposes of forced labor and sexual exploitation.[5]

INTRODUCTION

Project Rescue founders David and Beth Grant
had spoken to me about their work in India, but
it wasn't until I rode down Falkland Road in the
heart of Bombay's red-light district that I fully
understood the desperate need for their ministry.
Tiny prostituted girls—some appearing as young
as 10—lined the road soliciting potential male
customers. Dressed in colorful saris and adorned
with dangling earrings and bracelets, they could
be seen leading their customers into stalls shielded
by soiled curtains.

For many living in Bombay, prostitution is
culturally acceptable, though government officials
have taken steps to curtail the exploitation
of younger girls. Taxis, bicycles, rickshaws,
street vendors, and sidewalk cafes operate their
businesses surrounded by thousands of women
and girls in prostitution. For centuries prostitution
has thrived on Falkland Road, becoming part of
the city's appeal to international visitors.

According to Paul and Melodye Dixon, our
Project Rescue hosts, beyond the soiled curtains
are tunnels and stairways leading to thousands
of stalls. Women and children—all trapped in the
web of prostitution—lean out the windows of the
tall buildings as we drive by.

One young girl sees our vehicle and motions for us to stop. I ask if it's safe for us to step out of the car and explore on foot. Our driver says firmly, "No."

Later I learn that Westerners have been chased away with knives in this district, especially if the owners of the prostituted women suspect one is a journalist or investigator who could hurt their business.

I glance over at my 17-year-old daughter, Lindsay, who is noticeably perplexed by this awful scene. This is her first visit to a developing country like India, where dire poverty and abuse abound.

"Dad," she says, "these girls are about the same age as my sisters."

"It's tragic," I reply. "It's hard to believe this is really happening to these girls."

Falkland is dimly lit, although automobile headlights in bumper-to-bumper traffic serve as eerie spotlights on the girls. Amid the incessant honking and shouting from mobs of shoulder-to-shoulder pedestrians, anger rises in me. I'm reminded that these girls are not sex-slaves by choice; they are victims of greed, lust, prejudice ... and kidnapping.

Falkland Road is an epicenter of exploitation, I tell myself. Here human life is devalued. The weak are preyed upon. The defenseless are devoured.

CHILDREN OF PROSTITUTED WOMEN

As despair threatens to wrench tears from my eyes, we enter the compound of an innocuous stucco building. I'm informed that we are about to meet some of the children of women in prostitution who live under Bombay Teen Challenge (BTC)* and Project Rescue's care. We're ushered up three flights of stairs to an open room. As we pass through the door, nearly 100 smiling children break into applause. Sitting in neat rows on the floor, they await their teacher's instructions. She asks them to introduce themselves to us. One after another, they come and shake our hands and politely tell us their names:

"Asa."

"Buta."

"Nita."

"David."

As the string of names and handshakes continues, I am struck by how fortunate these children are. They have escaped the brothel to a place where they have a bed, clothing, food, water and medical care. In addition, they are being educated and learning about Jesus. Not to mention the genuine love and care they are receiving from the workers.

But what about the thousands who wait outside the walls of this compound? I ask myself. *What*

*about the children who live in their mothers' stalls
and have no way out? What needs to happen so
they can be rescued, too?*

Some of the children are so frail I could lovingly
cradle them in one arm, like I had each of my
four daughters when they were infants. But these
children are much older and should be larger and
stronger by now.

I ask the teacher if any of these children have
AIDS. She nods her head. "Yes ... many."

It's difficult to comprehend that some of these
children will not live long enough to experience
adulthood.

The head teacher invites the children to perform
a special song. They stand to attention like choir
members awaiting the signal from the conductor.
She pushes the play button on an old cassette
recorder and six young girls step out and dance to
the music.

FROM THE STREETS

The teacher interprets the lyrics for us. "They're
singing, 'Without His love we are nothing; we
have nothing without His love.'"

I'm suddenly fighting tears of gratitude, for these
children have truly been rescued from the clutches
of the enemy. No longer does he have reign over

their lives. No longer can he threaten their futures
with poverty, disease and abuse.

The teacher asks three of the children to step
forward and share their testimony.

The first boy says that he was living alone in
the streets when he was 10. He was taking drugs,
using alcohol, and sniffing glue to take away
his hunger pangs. Stealing became a way of life.
K.K. Devaraj, director of BTC-Project Rescue
in Bombay, found the boy at a train station
and brought him to the center. The boy says he
committed his life to Jesus three years ago at the
center and wants to follow Him the rest of his life.
"I love Jesus," he says, "because He found me and
saved me."

A 9-year-old girl approaches and speaks to
us with the poise of an adult. She points to her
sister who also resides at the center. Her mother
is enslaved in prostitution and, before she came
to the center, she was forced to beg for food and
money on the streets. She says Jesus changed her
life and gave her hope.

When the center first started, the teacher says,
the children would go back to their mothers each
morning and live under their beds in the stalls.
But now they live in the center year-round. Their
mothers are permitted to come and visit their
children twice a month.

The teacher says, "Many times the children
are in tears as they pray for their mothers. They

want them to know Jesus like they do. They realize where they came from and are filled with gratitude that the Lord has saved them."

Lindsay and I are invited to pray for the children. I ask them to express their appreciation to their teachers, K.K. Devaraj, the Dixons, and the Grants for their love and compassion.

The children again erupt in applause.

A MEMORABLE PRAYER

As I begin to pray, the children raise their hands and fervently seek the Lord like teenagers at a youth rally in the States. I can sense God's powerful presence. It's as though God is sitting on His throne with His eyes fixed on this upper room. These children have experienced the power of prayer and the miraculous work of God at an early age.

The teacher asks the children to pray for Lindsay and me. The children promptly gather around and lay their hands on us. A young girl prays with authority, thanking God for bringing us to visit them. She asks the Lord to protect us and to use our lives to help other children in India.

As we gather our things to leave, the children surround us to say goodbye. Some won't settle for handshakes—they prefer hugs. I'm reminded that some of these children have never felt the embrace of a parent.

As we descend the steps, I thank the Lord for having such love for these children that He called David and Beth Grant, K.K. Devaraj, and others to begin the work of Project Rescue. As a result, thousands of lives are being saved and hope has returned to the red-light district of Falkland Road.

In the days following, I would meet dozens of formerly prostituted women whose lives were changed by the power of Christ and the compassion of His followers. I met madams who left their brothels to pursue a relationship with Christ. I interviewed Project Rescue workers who dedicated their lives to offering the hope of salvation and the promise of a new life to prostituted women and their children.

Three days in Bombay left me with a myriad of emotions and questions.

The sex-slave trafficking crisis was no longer something I could ignore; now it had a face. Thousands of young, innocent faces. I understood why David and Beth Grant and others felt compelled to travel across the United States and around the world to rally believers to the cause of rescuing girls from the clutches of the enemy.

Project Rescue is fulfilling the mandate of Isaiah 58:6: "Is not this the fast that I have chosen? to loose the bands of wickedness, to undo the heavy burdens, and to let the oppressed go free, and that ye break every yoke?"(KJV).

Beyond the Soiled Curtain is a call to action. As famed missionary David Livingstone said, "Sympathy is no substitute for action." It's my prayer when readers set this book down that they will pick up this baton and ask the Lord what He would have them do to rescue girls and women for eternity.

This book will make some readers angry; it will cause others to shed tears of sorrow. But, more importantly, may it provoke believers to recommit themselves to the Great Commission, to rescuing the perishing and raising their voices in this global outcry against injustice.

—Hal Donaldson

*Bombay Teen Challenge (BTC) is a ministry of Teen Challenge International. BTC partners with Project Rescue in restoring and rescuing victims of sexual-slavery in Bombay.

"The most terrible poverty is loneliness and the feeling of being unloved."[1]

—Mother Teresa

CHAPTER ONE

SATURDAY NIGHT

As the blistering sun descended in Bombay, India, the city's red-light district awakened. Like mannequins in department store windows, thousands of young women adorned in bright-colored saris and jewelry took their positions on the streets. Their madams and owners lurked nearby, ensuring that the girls were working hard to lure would-be customers. For the girls, not meeting the day's quota could result in food deprivation, torture and incarceration.

Fifteen year-old Sumi peeled back the soiled curtain of her stall on Falkland Road. She peered at a middle-aged customer and watched as he handed the madam payment for her services. The young girl, a sex-slave for 6 years now, hoped that this customer—her ninth—would be the final one of the day. She prayed that business would be slow and the madam would release her from her stall to attend the Saturday evening church service conducted by BTC-Project Rescue.

Four young women, including Sumi, greeted us at the door of the church in the red-light district. Three of the girls were sold into prostitution by their parents. The other woman, slightly older, was once the madam of a brothel. After finding Christ, she bought her way out of the profession and began working with Project Rescue. The three girls have become regulars at the Saturday evening service, although they have not been fortunate enough to find a way out of the brothel.

"Hello, ladies," Beth Grant said, admiring their orange, red and yellow saris.

The four women smiled widely.

"Hi, Auntie and Uncle," they replied.

David Grant nodded.

For girls like Sumi, the Saturday church service is a reprieve from the shackles of abuse and neglect.

Lively music erupted inside the church rented by Project Rescue and Bombay Teen Challenge every Saturday night. The girls filed inside behind us and found a seat.

Ceiling fans were working hard to battle the heat, but the perspiration still formed beads on our brows. Every pew was filled—mostly with women who were formerly or currently enslaved. Some of the girls were kidnapped in Nepal, transported to Bombay, and forced into the business. Some were sold by their parents to procurers because they needed money to buy food and seed for their crops. And others came to Bombay with the false promise of an education and good-paying job. Regardless of their respective stories, they were not in prostitution by choice. Although they were all daughters of God, they were also victims of men.

As the service commenced, the lyrics "Holy Spirit, we welcome You in this place" bounced off the walls and reverberated throughout the community into the very brothels from which these girls had come.

The worship team was led by a young man, Steven, who ministered from his wheelchair. He came to Bombay years earlier looking for an Eastern religion that could heal him of his paralysis. He encountered K.K. Devaraj, director of BTC-Project Rescue. Devaraj said he could not promise physical healing, but he could promise the young man spiritual healing. Steven accepted the Lord and ever since has been working alongside Devaraj.

Steven invited the women to come forward if they wanted special prayer. More than half in attendance made their way to the front.

The children of the prostituted women, who live at the Project Rescue center, were seated as a group on the left side of the sanctuary. Several were filled with gratitude as they saw their mothers coming for special prayer.

One small child trailed her mother all the way

to the front.

PRAYER LINE

Some of the older women also came forward. Once these women have lost their usefulness in the brothels, they are discarded like unwanted clothing. Many victims of sexual slavery die of AIDS before they reach 40. Those who survive are relegated to a life of poverty, living on the streets scavenging for food and pure drinking water.

An estimated 5 million people live in the streets of Bombay, and thousands of them were formerly prostituted. They sleep on the sides of roads and in hovels. Meanwhile, some parts of the city boast state-of-the art shopping centers and high-rise corporate buildings. Bombay is a city where the rich and poor co-exist, where Mercedes and rickshaws can be seen side-by-side.

Some of the older women who shuffled forward for special prayer were living in the streets. Their clothing was tattered and frayed; their skin was wrinkled and parched from exposure to the sun day after day. But the women knew they were safe here; God did not see their outside. He was looking on their hearts. Their hands were raised in prayer to the God who gave them hope. Some were undoubtedly praying that God would liberate them from the tyranny of their past and the pain of their present.

K.K. Devaraj and his wife, Latijia, were among those who were anointing the women with oil. Some are wiping tears from their eyes with scarves that, out of tradition, covered their heads every time they entered a church.

In contrast, one of the young women who remained behind in her pew was dressed in a beautiful sari. Her dark hair was tied in a neat ponytail and her copper skin was silky smooth. It was obvious that someone—perhaps a madam or brothel owner—had taken very good care of her. Her eyes were closed as if praying or trying to deal with the burning questions associated with her life. Perhaps she dreaded what she would face when she returned to the brothel following the service.

Two women came to the service carrying their newborns against their chests. Most of the time they do not know who the father is; they just know it is one of many strangers who have paid for their services. The mother can only hope the infant was not infected with HIV.

The prayer session continued for more than half an hour. No one was in a hurry. The women had no desire to rush back to the brothels. There were no desserts, television episodes or loving families awaiting them.

When the women returned to their pews, the music exploded with the sounds of tambourine, drums and electric piano. Everyone was clapping and singing, "We are happy at the feet of Jesus. The devil is running away because God is giving us victory." Children were dancing in the aisles. One young man, once addicted to drugs and alcohol, was on his face crying out to God. The child of a sex-slave, he was studying to become a minister.

The joy that filled the sanctuary was a stark contrast to the misery of the brothel. Here these women were trophies of God's grace. In the brothels they were merely objects to satisfy the lust of men. Here they celebrated God's grace and mercy. There they endured insults and abuse.

Steven began singing lyrics that had deep meaning to each of these women: "The curse on us has been broken and now we are chasing the enemy away."

A man lumbered in during the music and squeezed into the back row. His clothes were dirty and his hair disheveled. But even if he's drunk or high on drugs, he was welcome here. Devaraj and his team are experienced at dealing with men and women who were battling addictions.

THE MESSAGE

Devaraj stepped to the microphone to deliver the evening message as he had many times before.

The women's eyes were fixed on their pastor and the wooden cross fastened to the wall behind him.

"Jesus loves you," Devaraj preached. "He gave *His* life so you might have eternal life with Him in heaven. He is here right now. He knows what you're going through and He will help you make it. Trust Him. Pray to Him every day. Surrender your life to Him. Let Him heal you. Let Him bless you and your children. He will give you peace, hope and strength."

As the message concluded, Devaraj invited the women to come forward for salvation and healing. No coaxing or manipulation was necessary. Immediately the pews emptied and the front of the sanctuary was filled with men and women wanting a touch from God. This night five women and one man received Jesus Christ as their personal Savior.

Seated a few rows in front of us, a teenage girl dressed in blue jeans and a fashionable blouse cautiously entered the prayer line. She hadn't actively participated in the worship service, although she listened intently to the message. She was among those who accepted Christ.

At the close of the service, Communion was served. Many of the women partook, but others refrained. Although they have received Christ's gift of forgiveness and chosen to follow Him, they feel they cannot partake of the emblems of Christ's sacrifice until they are liberated from the brothels.

We've learned that salvation here is often a process. The women are on a journey to Christ, away from their cultural religions and superstitions. The layers of bondage must be stripped away, which sometimes takes time. The emotional scars are deep and the demonic influence heavy. Prayer for deliverance is a frequent occurrence when a girl begins attending the weekly church services.

We wish it were as simple as raiding the brothels and escorting victims to safety. But such actions are dangerous. They would place the victims and Project Rescue workers at risk. Instead we have learned to take a long-term approach, believing that the love of Jesus will reach into the brothels and find a way to help the women and their children escape their life of bondage and begin a new life in one of the ever-expanding Project Rescue homes.

MIDNIGHT CALL

In 1997, David received a phone call in the middle of the night from K.K. Devaraj. He had held church services in the red-light district of Bombay and many women asked him to take their children from the brothels and give them a better life. A tearful Devaraj asked David if they could start a children's center. David sensed God was saying "Yes." That was the beginning of Project Rescue. The first center was started that year in Bombay, where children would have their physical and spiritual needs met. They would be cared for as if they were our own. At the time we did not know what God had in store for us and Project Rescue, but we soon realized this was the ministry for which He had been preparing us for many years.

MARRIAGE PROPOSAL

When Beth's first husband, Brian, died, she became a widow at 25. She was on the pastoral staff at a church in Wilmington, Delaware.

David had gone to India at 21 and worked with missionary legends Mark and Huldah Buntain. At 17, David promised God he would give every day and every dollar to the Lord's work. He vowed not to marry until he was at least 30, so he could devote himself to missions.

David and Brian were friends. So, for more than a year after Brian's death, David phoned Beth regularly to ensure that she was all right.

One night David prayed, "Lord, I'm willing to remain single the rest of my life. But if it's your will for me to get married, I have a recommendation. There's a young widow in Wilmington named Beth that I'd like to marry."

That night he sensed that God was blessing the desire of his heart. He phoned his father, saying, "Dad, I'm getting married."

"To who?" David's father asked.

"Well, I haven't seen her in a year. And the last time I saw her, she was married. Her husband died. But I'm flying up to ask her to marry me."

Shortly thereafter, David found himself on a flight to Philadelphia so we could have lunch together.

Sitting across the table from Beth, David said, "I know this is going to sound strange, but I've been praying that if it's God's will I'd like to marry you. This isn't really an official proposal. I'm just here to sort of stake out the land, so if anyone comes along you can tell them you are already spoken for."

A surprised Beth replied, "You're entitled to your opinion."

Undeterred, David promised to write her every day from India to demonstrate that he was serious.

Six months later, David officially proposed. And nine weeks later they were married and on the way to India.

VALUE OF A WOMAN

The first time David stepped to the pulpit in

India to introduce his wife, he announced that Beth had been a widow. He could almost hear the collective gasp from the audience. Even some of the pastors were alarmed. In some traditional Indian cultures, the widow's life is considered finished. She is an outcast, a bad omen. Her very presence indicates death. Her identity was lost when her husband died. And if she has no son whom she can serve, she is cursed.

The following morning, David met with the leadership team and pastors. He read Scriptures where God promised to provide for and protect the widow. The power of God fell on that room. Pastors began to weep and ask forgiveness. They promised to care for the widow as God had commanded them—not as the culture taught.

Over time the value of women in the church changed. Beth became a symbol of strength and newfound worth to women in the church in India.

Through the years, some pastors in India have said they were praying that David and Beth would have a son. In response, David would say, "No, ask God to give me daughters." This became an example to many in India.

So, when God called them to Project Rescue and the work of delivering girls from the bondage of prostitution, it was a natural progression. They had already begun the quest to champion the value of daughters and women—to help others see them as God sees them.

Together with K.K. Devaraj, they launched Project Rescue in Bombay in 1997. Little did they know what God had in store for the ministry. They just knew these children were precious to God and hundreds of thousands needed to be rescued and introduced to the Savior.

"Human life is the gift of our Creator—and it should never be for sale."

"It takes a special kind of depravity to exploit and hurt the most vulnerable members of society."

"Human traffickers rob children of their innocence; they expose them to the worst of life before they have seen much of life."

"Traffickers tear families apart. They treat their victims as nothing more than goods and commodities for sale to the highest bidder."[1]

—George W. Bush

CHAPTER TWO

AMMA'S LEGACY

Amy Carmichael, better known in India as Amma (which in Tamil means mother), was a pioneer in ministry to sex-slaves. Though she started her ministry more than 100 years ago, she is the one whose path we followed into the work of helping young girls trapped in sexual slavery.

Historically sex was a form of worship. Sometimes it was even required. A man would have sex every day as part of his daily worship. It was not unusual for a man to go to the local temple to have sex. Families gave a daughter to the temple, normally at the age of 12, as an offering to the gods. In doing so, they believed they would be blessed.

Many girls were sexually enslaved, and still are, at much younger ages. Some girls, then and now, are as young as 7 years old.

In 1901 a little girl named Preena lived in a southern Indian village. Like most children she loved to run through the village playing with the other children. But on this day she was not running for fun; she was running for her life ... and to retain her innocence. The men in pursuit wanted her for sex.

With her hands cupped and clutched toward her chest, her cool tears splashed down on the fresh burns she had just sustained. She knew this pain well. Once before, her hands had been branded when she ran away.

Desperate for help, the sobbing child made her way to a small church. There, she found refuge in the arms of a woman she only knew as Amma. Though Preena had no idea where Amma, an Irish missionary, came from, she felt safe and secure. But the feelings were fleeting.

"Bring the girl out," an angry knot of villagers demanded. "She is ours."

The confrontation with the villagers would set Carmichael's life and ministry on a new course. She had come to India to spread the gospel. But as she stood in defense of the little girl she realized that the best way to do that was through protecting Preena. Boldly, she refused to turn Preena over to the villagers.

Soon after, Carmichael began to take more children into her care. Within 12 years she was caring for 133 children and had founded Dohnavur Fellowship in the southern tip of India. For the next 55 years of her life Carmichael rescued nearly 1,000 children from situations

similar to that of Preena. "Sometimes it was as if
I saw the Lord Jesus Christ kneeling alone, as He
knelt long ago under the olive trees," Carmichael
wrote. "And the only thing that one who cared
could do, was to go softly and kneel down beside
Him, so that He would not be alone in His sorrow
over the little children."[2]

Such an evocative picture was characteristic of
Carmichael's writings, which grew to include 35
books translated into 15 languages. Where other
well-known English writers, such as Kipling and
Forrester, captured the rich tapestry of Indian
life, Carmichael brought to life the spiritual issues
among the sub-continent's millions of residents.

While Carmichael attended to an array
of needs among impoverished children, she
concentrated much of her efforts on rescuing the
young temple prostitutes. Known as *devadasi*,
these girls were sold by their families to local
temples and "married" to Hindu gods. The term
devadasi means "god's servants." In centuries
past, *devadasi* were celibate and performed
ceremonies and chores at the temples. But their
role degenerated to that of sex-slaves.[3]

By the sixth century A.D., the practice of
dedicating girls to Hindu gods was entrenched.
Carmichael arrived in India in 1895 and soon
discovered the practice during her itinerant
ministry among the outlying villages of Bangalore.
It broke her heart to discover young girls being

horribly abused with the consent of their families and communities. As a follower of Christ, she knew she had to help them.

REALITY CHECK

Similar practices, like those Amy encountered, still exist in brothels throughout Southern Asia. Horrible atrocities, such as rape and torture, continue to be forced on young girls. The perverse practice of sexual slavery violates every aspect of the victim, leaving near-total devastation in its wake. It's not just her body—it's her emotions; it's her mind; it's her spirit—they all have been traumatized, leaving little semblance of normality. For a ministry to be effective, it must address each and every dimension of the person. Jesus did this. His ministry was holistic, reaching the body, the heart, mind, and spirit. With Jesus as our model, Project Rescue strives to do the same.

In many ways, Project Rescue and other organizations with similar missions are just carrying on Amma's work. Yet, like a pandemic, the sexual slavery of young girls is spreading. To stem the tide, it will require that we acknowledge the problem and educate ourselves. It will require us to take a stand against the forces of evil and prayerfully rely upon the power of the Holy Spirit.

And it will require Christians, governments and agencies to discover ways to work together.

A YOUNG BRIDE

Durgamma was 12 years old on her wedding day. Through the whitewashed arches of the Uligamma temple, Durgamma proudly marched toward the banks of India's Thungabadra river. The eyes of her relatives, friends, and neighbors were fixed on the young bride.

Close to an overhead bridge spanning the Thungabadra, a priest accepted the goat brought by Durgamma's family. With a quick stroke of a blade, he sacrificed the animal to the temple goddess Uligamma. The goat's blood dripped into the river where hundreds of worshipers were bathing.

Durgamma patiently submitted to her women relatives who applied a sandalwood paste to her body and bathed her in the river. After they dressed her in a white sari and blouse, she listened to the high caste priest chant and pray in Sanskrit, the ancient language of Hindu scriptures. As his prayers concluded, the priest sprinkled a yellowish mixture of turmeric paste and water over her head and she felt the refreshingly cool liquid trickle down her back.

Durgamma walked up to the temple where a priest put a glittering string of red and white beads strung on saffron-colored thread around her neck. No groom, however, came to meet this bride. Durgamma was being wed to the temple goddess; her life would be spent as a *devadasi*, a temple prostitute. Uligamma's spirit, the priests teach, has entered Durgamma's body. For the rest of her life, when priests and other men sleep with her, it is not Durgamma, but the goddess they are sleeping with. It is the goddess' desires that the men must appease.[4]

"This simple word, *devadasi*," Dr. I.S. Gilada, one of India's most prominent AIDS activists and an honorary secretary of the Indian Health Organization, told World Vision, "is a label which condemns 5,000 to 10,000 girls every year into a life of sexual servitude and subsequently into prostitution."[5]

In Carmichael's day, the wedding ritual was far more prominent than it is today and she battled it at great personal risk. Once Carmichael rescued a 5-year-old girl from a temple, but was caught doing so. Carmichael faced a seven-year prison sentence, but miraculously the charges were dropped without explanation.

She faced other challenges that ranged from angry confrontations to a debilitating health condition called neuralgia, an affliction of the nerves that caused great weakness and kept her bedridden for weeks at a time. While physical illness and confrontations can arise in most people's lives, Amy was convinced that she was at war with a spiritual enemy intent on derailing God's plans to rescue young girls from temple prostitution.

"David and Beth, we must go down this road," said lifelong India missionary Andrew McCabe when we told him of our vision for Project Rescue. "But I must tell you, there is nothing more demonized and dark in this nation than this. If we go down this road, all hell will break loose. This endeavor may cost you everything, but, as you know, it is God's heart that we do His will no matter how difficult the challenge."

As Andrew McCabe predicted, within days of launching Project Rescue, we encountered spiritual warfare that threatened to bring the ministry to a halt.

THE ACCIDENT

Beth and our daughters were set to fly back to Brussels, Belgium, from Bangalore, India, after our meeting with McCabe and other personnel. As we had done many times before, we piled their luggage into the van and climbed in. I accompanied the family to the airport—even though I was remaining in Bangalore for a short time.

We were driving at normal speeds and scanning the road for pedestrians, carts, or motorcycles that might dart out in front of us as commonly happens in India. To the side of the road, I spotted a little boy and a girl waiting to cross. They appeared old enough to know not to run out in front of the cars. Somehow, children in developing nations have an innate ability to wander close to danger or traffic without getting injured.

Thunk. It was a sickening sound, the kind that only comes when a human body is dropped on pavement or hit by fast-moving machinery.

Our driver slammed on his brakes and pulled to the side of the road. Beth grabbed our daughters and pushed them to the floorboard and began to pray.

Though we didn't know what or who we hit, we both knew immediately the gravity of our situation—for both the child and ourselves. We knew from news accounts that people had been beaten and vehicles torched at accident scenes for running over a child.

I jumped out of the van to see what or whom we had hit. My heart sank when I recognized the little girl who had been standing on the side of the road. She was no more than 4 years old.

As I huddled with others over the little girl, a murmur of disbelief emanated from them. Her family members ran their hands over her tiny body checking for broken bones, cuts, bumps ...

anything to find her injuries. She did not appear
to be in pain.

"She is okay," announced one of the men.
"There is nothing wrong with her."

An old man who had been standing in the
median the entire time said to me, "Sir, you have
just seen the work of God."

Stunned, I could only find a single word:
"Amen."

I climbed back in the van thanking God for
sparing the girl's life. Without saying it, we both
knew the spiritual warfare had begun and God
had prevailed. We knew He had supernaturally
intervened. The battle to spare thousands of girls'
lives through Project Rescue was on.

AMY AT REST

Amy Wilson Carmichael, after 55 years of
service, went to be with the Lord on January 18,
1951. She was buried in her garden next to some
of the children she had rescued, who had later
died of disease. Although she requested that no
tombstone be placed over her grave, her children
situated a bird bath over it containing one word:
"Amma."

Amma dedicated her life to serving the children
of India. It was a calling that required much
sacrifice, commitment, and reliance on God.

She knew she was at war with the powers of darkness. Those of us who walk in her footsteps have entered the same fight for the victims of the sex-slave industry. We too are at war with an enemy who enslaves girls and attacks those who come to their rescue. Like Amy, we pray for God's protection, guidance and blessing every day. This is not a casual ministry to be approached lightly. This is a no-holds-barred battle for the lives of women and girls who cannot fight for themselves.

"I've seen the results of this horrific violation of human rights. I remember meeting a young girl who had been sold by her family and taken to a brothel where she was forced into prostitution. And when she escaped and returned home, she was sold again. When she contracted AIDS and was too sick to work, she was turned out of the brothel, made her way home, was turned away again and died in a house of refuge for girls like herself."[1]

—*Hillary Rodham Clinton*

CHAPTER THREE

A GLOBAL TRAGEDY

In 1997, David received the phone call that would change our view of the world. K.K. Devaraj had taken a Bombay Teen Challenge outreach team into the Falkland Road red-light district of Bombay to hold church services. As they sang and shared the story of Christ's love, more than 100 young women indicated a desire to follow Jesus. Devaraj discovered a horrifying world none of us knew existed. Block after block of multistoried buildings housed more than 50,000 women and girls. Many of them had been sold into sexual slavery by their parents. Some were from families in poverty-stricken villages in bordering Nepal; they had been trafficked to Bombay when they were children.

As Devaraj and the team made their way through the dismal surroundings, women begged them to take their small daughters to safety away from Falkland Road, so they would not be forced into prostitution as well.

"You are our only hope," one woman pleaded with Devaraj as she held out an infant girl. "Please, you must take her!"

Returning to his office, a tearful Devaraj called David.

"Could we open a safe home for 37 little girls?" he asked, heartbroken from this eye-opening experience. "Many of these girls have been born in the brothels. A home could be their only means to escape the same fate as their mothers."

David paused, whispering a prayer for God's guidance.

"I don't know what this will cost," David replied, "but we must do it. God would want us to do this. Yes, let's start a home."

Embarking on this new challenge, we began an exhaustive research project that led to more stunning revelations. We soon learned this was a cruel and ruthless industry that had no regard for human life. And it had mushroomed into a global tragedy. The ministry that would eventually become known as Project Rescue had begun.

ECONOMICS

Trafficking in persons, especially women and children, for the purpose of sexual exploitation is quickly becoming the world's fastest growing

industry and most profitable criminal activity.
According to the Trafficking in Persons Report
from the U.S. Department of State, it is likely
that virtually every nation in the world is engaged
to some extent in this tragic trade, whether as
a country of origin, transit or destination of
victims. UNICEF estimates that 2 million children
are forced, sold, abducted or coerced into the
commercial sex trade annually. Estimates of
individuals trafficked across international borders
each year range anywhere from 800,000 to 4
million.[2] And the United States is not isolated
from this scourge. The U.S. State Department
estimated in 2006 that as many as 17,500 men,
women and children are trafficked into the nation
each year, many for sexual exploitation.[3]

Human trafficking has exploded into a
$32-billion-a-year global industry with sexual
trafficking constituting a major part.[2] A girl who
is purchased by a trafficker for as little as $150
can be sold to customers as many as 10 times a
night and bring in $10,000 a month.[4]

With minimal expenses, some police as co-
predators, an almost unlimited number of victims
to prey upon, and a large market, trafficking for
sexual exploitation is surpassing the sale of illegal
drugs as the preferred industry for criminals.

Sexual trafficking may be defined as the
movement of women and children, within
national or across international borders, for

the purpose of prostitution or other forms of commercial sexual exploitation. It includes the recruitment, transportation, harboring, transfer, or sale of women and children for these purposes. The ultimate end of sexual trafficking is brutality, sexual slavery and, not infrequently, death.

Unfortunately, the chaos of current political, economic and social factors in our world has created a ripe environment for ruthless traffickers who prey on vulnerable victims. This is vividly illustrated by nations that were formerly part of the Soviet Union, where one-third of all sexual trafficking in the world occurs.[5] The economic and moral upheaval that followed the U.S.S.R.'s collapse created an atmosphere where staggering numbers of young women and girls who live in poverty are easily lured by procurers' false promises of lucrative jobs in Western Europe. Others are abducted outright in Moldova, Romania and Bulgaria as they walk from school or on remote roads.[6] In Moldova, in particular, a despicable pattern of trafficking targets the thousands of girls who live in state orphanages and are released as teenagers. Traffickers know the exact timing of the release of the 16- and 17-year-old orphans; they are there to meet them when they leave and have nowhere to go. In all of the trafficking schemes, once a victim's legal papers come into the possession of their new boss, they quickly lose their freedom and any illusions of a better life. Enslavement follows in brothels in cities across Western Europe where new victims are raped and brutalized until they are willing to submit.

FOR SALE

In a hillside village in Nepal, a father brought his 10-year-old daughter to a meeting with a procurer. The girl smiled, but she was shy and hid behind her shawl when spoken to. The procurer, a woman in her mid-40s, surveyed the girl with well-trained eyes. She knew what men were looking for.

"She is very beautiful."

The father nodded.

"Are you willing to work?" the woman asked the girl.

The girl smiled.

"Tell her you will work," snapped the father, obviously irritated that she had not answered. "She is a hard worker ... a very hard worker."

The woman peered at the girl skeptically. An awkward silence fell. Fearing he might lose the deal, he shot his daughter a quick look. "Tell her you are a hard worker!"

The girl nodded.

"Will you be willing to do anything?" the woman asked.

"Yes, she will do anything," the father replied.

The woman leaned close to the girl's face and looked her in the eyes. The girl shuddered, then cowered.

"Will you do anything we tell you to do?"

The father nudged the girl.

"Yes," said the girl in halting innocent obedience.

The woman and the father discussed terms. She handed him a stack of bills. He carefully counted the money, then, without emotion, released his daughter to the woman.

The girl had been told she would be given a job in a Bombay factory. She would earn enough money to live a good life, and still send money back to her family. Doing so would not only help her family, but would also increase her worth in the eyes of her father. Unbeknownst to the girl—and possibly even to her father—an honorable job was not awaiting her. She was destined for Bombay, to be enslaved, brutalized, and repeatedly raped. And, most likely, to be infected with HIV. The deal her father cut was her death sentence.

Such scenes are played out daily throughout Nepal and other impoverished countries. From the small poverty-stricken villages of Nepal alone, parents sell 7,000-9,000 young daughters a year into sexual slavery to the brothels of India. Parents eagerly purchase relief from their daily quest for survival. In exchange their daughters are condemned to a living nightmare, most often followed by an early death.

According to research by Kevin Bales, extreme poverty is where slavery grows best:

- Wars and natural disasters around the world create women and children refugees who are especially vulnerable to victimization as they flee for their lives.

- Globalization has facilitated the transport of goods and services across international borders, including the transport of human cargo and sexual services.

- Times of political upheaval are accompanied by the upheaval of traditional family and community support systems. Presumed protectors become predators, and the human rights of the weakest and most vulnerable are savagely trampled with little to no recourse.

- Within [some] traditional cultures, women and daughters are viewed as property, financial liabilities, social burdens and even children of a lesser god. As a result, daughters and wives may be neglected, underfed, undereducated, abused and sold as property. Their primary significance as a person is derived from their relationship with the male members of their families, whether fathers, husbands or sons. A woman's value is associated with her ability to bear a child, particularly a male child. Her life and future are to great extent in the hands of men.

- The burgeoning global appetites for child sex, homosexuality, pornography and sex tourism are creating an insatiable demand for sex-slaves.

- With the global AIDS crisis, affluent customers looking for sexual services with virgins are driving the market for younger and younger victims.[7]

If the injustice of trafficking and sexual slavery were not sufficiently deplorable, the tragedy is compounded as victims are routinely victimized in the court and law enforcement systems of the world. Often when trafficked women are taken in the police raids of brothels, they are treated as criminals or illegal immigrants. They are frequently charged and imprisoned or deported to face an uncertain fate in their own countries. Meanwhile, most of the traffickers and pimps remain free to prey on new victims.

TWO MILLION MINORS

Overall, an estimated 2 million minors are currently enslaved in the global commercial sex trade. The growing demand for younger victims is fueled by American and European businessmen engaged in "sex-tourism," Africans and Asians who believe that intercourse with a virgin will cure them of AIDS or prosper their businesses, and pedophiles from around the world.

Lucrative profits of the sex trade have made it attractive to organized crime. Crime syndicates actively lobby governments to legalize prostitution, which they claim will increase tax revenue. They also campaign for no restrictions on the World Wide Web, which has become an invaluable tool for prostitution and human trafficking. Young girls and women are advertised like new cars, complete with photographs and profiles. The crime syndicate's propaganda also falsely claims that the legalization of prostitution and Web "freedom" will reduce human trafficking and give women control over their own bodies. They fail to acknowledge that most women do not willingly choose prostitution. The lack of choices drives them to the business as a survival strategy and compels them to take risks, which makes them even more vulnerable to traffickers.

Many women in prostitution—especially in

developing nations where AIDS is rampant—die in their early 20s. But the voices of these victims are seldom heard. Their stories are not seen on *60 Minutes*. They suffer in silence—in obscurity—while corrupt governments and organized crime prosper from their pain.

My Dream

I live here in the market place with no security.
Every day I face problems. I cannot sleep
peacefully at night, so I am sleepy all day. I get
scolding for that because people do not understand
why I doze during the day. People shout, ladies
fight and girls quarrel over small things. The place
is stinking and dirty. I cannot move freely as I
fear police may take me or some bad people may
pick me up and do bad things with me. I have no
freedom. I scream and groan inside for a better
place where I can live peacefully, where I can sleep
securely at night, move about freely, play with
friends, and go to school.

I dream of such a place where everyone loves
everyone and no one fights. The place will be neat
and clean. There will be playgrounds for us to
play. There will be a room of my own. I do not
like the girls and ladies standing here waiting for
men they do bad things with. Girls are brought
from villages and are sold here and forced to do
bad things. They are poor and helpless. Their
uncles, aunties or relatives sell them here. Girls
of my age are being abused every day. I am afraid
of this place. I want to live in a place where I will
have no fear.

Radha, age 11

"It is appalling that in the twenty-first century hundreds of thousands of women, children, and men made vulnerable by civil conflict, dire economic circumstances, natural disasters or just their own desire for a better life are trafficked and exploited for the purposes of sex or forced labor. The deprivation of a human being's basic right to freedom is an affront to the ideals of liberty and human dignity cherished by people around the world."[1]

—Colin L. Powell

CHAPTER FOUR

PORTRAIT OF A VICTIM

Manju looked like all the girls. She was petite, had tired eyes and her face was framed by long black hair. Perhaps if she had been born in another country to a wealthy, or even middle-class, family, her life would have turned out differently. Maybe then all she would have to worry about was making good grades, juggling extracurricular activities, and finding what she would wear to school tomorrow morning.

Sadly, that was not even near her reality. She had been kidnapped from her village, sold to a brothel, and had spent a great deal of her childhood being prostituted in Bombay.

Fortunately she found her way to one of Project Rescue's homes.

One afternoon she gathered with the other girls for a time of prayer.

"Lord, we praise You. Thank You for Your love," said one of the girls leading devotions that afternoon. "You are so good to us. Thank You for Your provisions, grace and love."

The other girls joined in and a chorus of prayers filled the room. Some of the girls simply raised their hands and praised the Lord with sweet, melodic tones. Others prayed forcefully on behalf of their mothers and friends who were incarcerated in the brothels. It was awe-inspiring to hear their voices ascend heavenward.

Manju suddenly placed her hands over her ears to block out their voices. Then she began writhing on the floor. The girls were frightened—but not Devaraj or his workers. They had seen this before. Whether one calls it demonic influence or mental illness, it was obvious Manju needed deliverance. Devaraj instructed everyone to pray.

"In the name of Jesus," Devaraj prayed, "we claim authority over this condition."

After 30 minutes of prayer, the convulsing stopped and Manju went limp.

"Jesus, Jesus, Jesus," she cried with tears streaming down her face. "I love You, Jesus."

That night Manju experienced the power of God. She was liberated from her past and given hope for a new beginning.

THE DEBT

Since human trafficking is an international, multi-billion-dollar enterprise, there aren't many major cities throughout the world unscarred by the tragedy. Within sight of the Eiffel Tower or the Sydney Opera House or even the Empire State Building, young women's lives are being sold piecemeal to a host of strangers intent on fulfilling their selfish, lustful desires.

While ministering in Rome, for example, we spoke with a local pastor whose congregation had taken it upon themselves to reach out to the African street walkers brought to the city under false pretenses. According to the pastor, thousands of African girls sell themselves in the streets of Rome to pay off their debt or buy their freedom from the Italian mafia. Though street life has a way of quickly hardening the hearts of such women, congregation members regularly invite them to church and offer to help them in tangible ways.

"I want to leave this way of life," confessed one of the teenage girls after she prayed at the church's altar. Tears quickly flooded her eyes and she crumpled into a heap. "But to do that I would have to come up with $35,000 to be released by the people who brought me here. That is the cost of my freedom. How will I ever make $35,000?"

The young woman's story is a familiar one. A

procurer coaxed her into leaving her homeland with promises of a good life, then turned her over to a brothel owner.

"Someone came to my village and told me I could make lots of money in Rome because I was so beautiful," she said. "The woman said I could come to Europe and become a model or a travel hostess. She said I would be paid more money than I had ever seen. I believed her. Now I sleep with many different men each night and make very little money."

In the poorest villages when visitors promise great wealth and an easy life, they are quickly believed. Eager to escape poverty, many parents willingly sell their daughters or enter into loans against their daughter's future earnings. In other words, they trade their daughters into a life of slavery in exchange for empty promises.

Americans find it difficult to understand how a parent could give a child away. But in many of the world's cultures, daughters are deemed inferior to sons. A son brings prestige and often a marriage dowry; a girl does not. A son can also help a family muscle its way to prosperity or at least out of the lowest cellar of poverty; girls usually cannot. A boy is seen as a blessing; a girl is simply seen as a burden.

It is not unusual in some Indian villages for couples to practice infanticide until they have a son. With girls commanding so little respect or value, parents often accept the procurer's offers. The money paid for a girl may be such a large sum to family members that it would take years for them to earn an equal amount.[2]

MULTITUDE OF FACTORS

There are many reasons that the sex-slave industry is expanding: poverty, disease, crime, disasters, war, caste systems, weak trafficking laws and more.

As the world's economy shifts, for example, poverty has threatened more regions outside Africa and Asia. With the breakdown of the former Soviet Union's economy, unemployment has skyrocketed. People who relied on the state for support have no jobs and nowhere to turn. There is no safety net. Because of this, families have no way to feed their children or even sustain themselves. These nations become fertile ground for sex-slave trafficking.

In countries where AIDS is taking the lives of more and more parents, the orphans often become victims of child predators. Anything that breaks up a family—divorce, natural disaster, war—gives opportunity for children to be forced into the worldwide currents of bartered human flesh.

In the aftermath of the southern Asia tsunami in 2004, for example, there were reports of pedophiles offering orphaned children food and clothing. With thousands of people killed across the region, it was easy to add living, healthy children to the enormous list of the missing. They became targets for kidnapping.

In regions where a social hierarchy encourages the strong to dominate the weak, that oppression often becomes sexual in nature. In Darfur, for example, there has been the systematic rape of village women and girls by the Sudanese militia known as the Janjaweed.

In India, the caste system is much weaker today, but historically it encouraged sexual exploitation. One low caste was required by tradition to present all of its women bare-breasted in public. This was to destroy any sense of pride or modesty and to demonstrate that a woman walking into a village uncovered was little more than an animal. She could be raped at any time by a higher caste male.

Yet sexual exploitation is not limited to India's castes. According to the U.S. State Department, sexual predators from the United States and European countries frequent countries like Thailand to evade the law in their own countries. The Department asserts that the child sex-tourism business is booming—and many Americans are involved.

Women and girls often find themselves under the brutal control of criminal organizations whose resources and ruthlessness appear limitless.

Knowing reprisal will be swift and cruel, most prostituted women refuse to entertain thoughts of running away. They are essentially trapped, having fallen into the clutches of opportunistic businessmen who are willing to kill or discard anyone who stands in the way of their profit. And, as the sex-slave trade continues to expand, more and more girls watch their dreams fade and their bitterness and fear rise.

EASY MONEY

Hollywood glamorizes prostitution. Tabloids focus their headlines on women in prostitution who are more than willing to expose johns at the right price. And publications purchase memoirs that portray an optimistic picture of prostitution. The stories read like fairy tales complete with an exciting life, charming men and lots of money. That image is far from reality. Life in prostitution is filled with remorse and regret. Abuse, rape, trauma on multiple levels, disease, addictions and eventually death are the authentic themes of prostitution.

Glamorized stories of prostitution have lured some women into the business. Some willfully sell their bodies for profit. But, worldwide, millions of women are not in prostitution by choice. They are literally slaves.

Attractive Asian prostituted women are transported to the United States to increase their earnings among American clientele. Women and children from around the world are regularly moved into the United States across the Mexican border to increase profits. This pipeline allows the gangs to make more money by rotating the women and advertising an exotic and ever-changing lineup of girls.[3]

EVIL AT WORK

No matter if they are in prostitution for the money, or because they are victims, the women are spiritually, emotionally and psychologically enslaved. Whether forced into prostitution or enticed by it, each woman lives in an environment where evil has full sway and is at work using and abusing that most personal element of a woman's identity. There can be no denying that the global sex trade has been fueled by unbridled sexual activity.

The Bible speaks of the power of sexuality, when misused, to pollute one's spirituality. When the Children of Israel neared the Promised Land they enjoyed a series of victories over Canaanite armies. The people of Moab knew they would be next and called on Balaam to prophesy against Israel (Numbers 22-24). When that ploy failed, the Moabites turned to sex. They invited the

Israelite men to have relations with Moabite women at religious festivals. As a result, Israel endured God's judgment (Numbers 25). In Romans 1, the bondage of sin in people's lives is manifested in sexual deviance. The apostle Paul notes the connection between sin, idolatry, false religions and perverted sexual behavior.

Sexual perversion is a reflection of the spiritual condition of one's heart. Today, in India, many express devotion to their religion through decadent sexual behavior and exploitation.

When we reach out to a woman or girl trapped in prostitution, we are not just working with an individual; we're combating an evil system, a set of sexual mores, generations of bondage, and a social structure that is thousands of years old. The system perpetuates itself, infecting every level of society and government. But we must never forget that caste systems and criminal syndicates are no match for the power of Christ's love. Jesus said, "I will build my church; and the gates of hell shall not prevail against it" (Matthew 16:18, KJV). The gates of hell have no clearer representation than the doorways and curtains of the world's brothels. Christians must unite in taking the love of Christ through those doors and freeing those within. For the millions of young women in India and many other countries, Jesus and His workers are their only hope for escape.

"For to be free is not merely to cast off one's chains, but to live in a way that respects and enhances the freedom of others."[1]

—Nelson Mandella

CHAPTER FIVE

A GIRL'S LIFE

Shila's large brown eyes constantly darted back
and forth across the room taking in everything
around her. She had a quick smile, friendly
demeanor and composure beyond her years. To
see Shila was to see what a bundle of energy looks
like wrapped in flesh and bone.

"I'm getting fat," she said to a female Project
Rescue care-giver.

"Shila, you're skinny," the worker responded. "I
doubt anyone would think of you as fat."

Shila placed her hands on her hips and grinned
mischievously. "I'm not skinny, I'm fa—."

"Oh yes you are," interrupted the care-giver.
"Your waist is the size of my leg."

Shila huffed. Though she knew she was thin
she had gained much weight since coming to the
Project Rescue home. She was very proud and
protective of every ounce she had gained.

"I used to be skinny, but now I'm fat," retorted
Shila, pushing her 11-year-old, ironing-board flat

stomach out. "See."

She pointed to her stomach as if it were convincing evidence. It wasn't. She was still rail thin, but compared to the day she came to us from the streets of Bombay where Devaraj found her, she looked much healthier.

"God has been good to you," the worker said.

Shila nodded.

"You should have seen me before I came here," said Shila quick to share her testimony with anyone who would listen. "When Uncle Devaraj found me I had been living on the streets, hungry and really thin. Now by God's grace I am fat."

BORN FEMALE

We have two daughters, Rebecca and Jennifer, who are healthy and grown. Our memories of their childhood and teen years are full of the typical highlights and joys. Like any dedicated parents, we can't imagine anything but the best for our girls. We would make any sacrifice to help them achieve their dreams and God's visions for their lives. Sadly, Satan has so blinded many parents in India and in other countries that they have come to see their daughters as collateral for making them money. A 2002 report on the community of Ratlam, India, described the common practice of devoting the oldest daughter

to prostitution to support the family. The tradition
is so ingrained that the girls accept their fate
without complaint.

"I knew what was in store for me when I was 5
years old," one girl said.[2] By age 12, the girls are
made available for prostitution. Fathers typically
set aside a room in the home for the business.
Imagine the distrust for a father that this creates
in a child. We find our identity in our earthly
fathers. That is why we endeavor to connect the
girls in our care to the Heavenly Father who *can*
be trusted. He will never betray them. Instead
He gives them His identity. To every girl who has
been relegated to being a commodity, God can
bring restoration and a new self-image. When that
happens, healing takes place.

THE INITIATION

Most parents cannot imagine allowing their
daughter to be harmed in any way. But in countries
where females are severely undervalued—and
even seen as liabilities that can bring a family to
ruin—it is no wonder they are so readily discarded.
The child never hears a gentle word or feels a
tender touch. That is the only life many girls
know.

Such a reality is made worse when parents
knowingly or ignorantly put an already neglected

girl into an assembly-line existence ... where her body is a throw-away object to be used multiple times every day. It is estimated that there are half a million children prostituted in India.

Young, once-innocent girls are forced to comply with the unnatural sexual demands of men old enough to be their fathers or even grandfathers. The girls are initiated first—brutalized to the point that they will choose daily sexual violation rather than cruel punishment for non-compliance. They are beaten, raped, starved, brutalized and traumatized into submission. In Thailand, for example, a fire broke out in a brothel. Five young girls burned to death. They couldn't escape because they had been chained to their beds. This brutality and abuse extends to the communities across America.

In America?

It doesn't seem possible, but it is.

Traffickers "break girls in" along the Mexican border. Women and girls are raped and brutalized for weeks until they no longer have any fight left in them. Then they are smuggled into the States.

The New York Times reported how a van would bring a young girl to a convenience store. Her handlers would give her a description of her customer. Then she would go into the store, walk up to the stranger and say, "Daddy, are you ready yet?"

That man would then walk out of the store with the girl, and she would never be seen again.

DRUGGED AND DELIVERED

Anita was 15 years old when a couple she trusted promised her a job. They convinced her there was an opportunity to work as a domestic helper, which would also afford her the chance to pursue her studies. The idea of a secure job was enticing, as it would be for any young girl in Nepal. Believing she could trust this couple, she left her home in pursuit of a brighter future.

The couple drugged Anita, then took her to a movie theater where a brothel owner met them. Two hundred dollars changed hands and Anita's future of forced prostitution was sealed. For the next 18 years she lived and worked in the red-light district of Bombay.

It was in the red-light district that she first heard the gospel from those serving on the Bombay Teen Challenge staff. Along with her brothel owner, she accepted Jesus into her life. Shortly thereafter, Anita was released from the brothel and was permitted to return to Nepal. She now lives at the Katmandu Home of Hope, where she is taking literacy and sewing classes. She has hopes of opening a tailoring shop of her own one day.

THE DARK SIDE

Even after a girl has accepted her cruel fate and become submissive to her handlers, her life is not any easier. Food is scarce in the brothels, hygiene is lacking, and lesbianism is rampant. Some women find solace and companionship in the arms of other women. It is there, if only for a few fleeting moments each day, that a girl might feel loved and accepted. Girls who disintegrate emotionally are sometimes thrown into the streets to die.

There is also a spiritual dimension to contend with. Beyond the human brutality the girls must endure, there is enormous spiritual darkness. Victims are open to the demonic forces that thrive in an environment like a brothel, where every form of immorality is celebrated. Scripture speaks of a slave girl in the city of Philippi (Acts 16:16-19). She was demon-possessed and exploited by her masters to tell fortunes. There are still spirits today that take control of young lives involved in prostitution. A girl may come out of a terrible physical environment and experience a degree of recovery, but until her spiritual issues are addressed she will never be completely free.

In some cases, girls will not let go of the spiritual darkness that binds them. They will begin life in one of our recovery homes and start to learn a new trade and grow in a relationship with Jesus only to leave the program and return to prostitution. They have lived with lies for so long, they cannot accept the truth.

Some prostituted women who have turned their children over to our care have later demanded the return of a child. This is heartbreaking to our ministry personnel. But it is a risk we are willing to take for the ones who remain in the program and progress to better lives.

Many children haunt the fringes of our ministry. They know of our outreaches. They come to our services. But they are still imprisoned within the walls of the brothels. That too is heartbreaking— because God has given us the capacity to care for many more children. But we find ourselves constrained by the need for additional resources and staff who know they are divinely called to this kind of ministry.

THE CHURCH

Jaya had been waiting patiently all night. Not one to verbalize her feelings, she could only shake her head in disgust as she awaited her final customer of the night.

"Please God, help me!" she prayed.

Suddenly the curtain to her closet-sized room was drawn back and in stepped a chubby, foreign man. He was ushered into the small room by one of the madams who gripped a small wad of cash in her hand—Jaya's price.

Jaya smiled at the man to satisfy him, but more to appease the madam.

"You will have a good time," said the madam to the man as he looked down on 14-year-old Jaya with lustful eyes and a sick grin. "She will do whatever you ask."

Jaya nodded in compliance. Though she would hate every second of the encounter, she would act quickly so she could get to the Falkland Road church service on time. There, she could receive prayer. Be encouraged. Raise her hands to her Savior and pray that He would rescue her from her circumstances. The life of the church service and the presence of God are a far cry from the oppressive, lifeless spirit of the brothel. Jaya lived for those two hours of freedom each week.

But this particular evening Jaya's customer lingered. He paid for another session. Jaya knew what this meant—she would miss church tonight. Seven days would pass before she could be in the presence of God where she could receive comfort and hope.

Loneliness and separation from the church set in. Jaya wanted to run away or fake an illness, but she knew the price would be too painful. They might burn her arms with cigarettes or withhold her food.

With tears welling in her eyes, she decided she had no choice but to agree to the customer's

demands. This night belonged to him. She
belonged to him.

THE SAVIOR'S TOUCH

For the most part, secular groups that try to
help sexually exploited women find emotional
healing have a low success rate. Meeting a girl's
physical needs doesn't guarantee she will be
released from spiritual bondage. If the spiritual
and emotional issues aren't dealt with, victimized
girls frequently find themselves back in the
brothels within weeks—if not days.

When a girl comes out of a brothel, it is
sometimes like looking into a dead person's eyes.
After all, something inside her mind and spirit
had to die in order for her to survive the horror.
Being raped daily leaves deep emotional scars.
Thus, the work of Project Rescue essentially
begins by walking with a dead person. Only faith,
intervention, and an encounter with Jesus Christ
bring girls back to life. But when that happens
you can see it in their eyes. We call it having the
eyes of death or the eyes of light. Our prayer is
that every girl will have eyes of light.

We have a duty to help save and protect these
girls from a dark world bent on destroying them.
We have a God-given responsibility to work at
preserving their hope.

It is too easy to relegate girls caught in prostitution to statistics. But it is crucial that every girl be recognized as a daughter—a daughter of God and a sister to every believer. Perhaps then —when we see them as members of God's family —we will be more inclined to make the sacrifices necessary to welcome them home.

"Defeating human trafficking is a great moral calling of our time."

"More and more countries are coming to see human trafficking for what it is—a modern-day form of slavery that devastates families and communities around the world."[1]

—Condoleezza Rice

CHAPTER SIX

'THE BOMBAY DISEASE'

For weeks Anju was curled up like a baby on her thin bed. Flesh clung to her bones like shrink wrap. Her breathing was labored and her agonizing pain was masked only by her clenched teeth.

Death was coming for Anju. Everyone knew it. Months ago, when AIDS began to manifest itself and customers refused to go near her, the brothel owner kicked her out into the street. We took her in.

For years Anju had been forced to sacrifice her body to countless men who did the most intimate and vile things to her, yet they never knew anything about her—only that she brought them pleasure. Her only reward was an incurable disease that was slowly racking her body.

It is estimated that as many as 60 percent of those prostituted in India are infected with HIV/AIDS.[2] One study reports that 70 percent of those prostituted in Bombay are HIV-positive.[3] That is why some call it "the Bombay disease." It is no surprise that Anju became infected and was subsequently discarded.

Many women in Anju's predicament wind up dying alone in the streets when they become too sick to comply. It is the perfect injustice for a life that has known nothing but injustice.

"A dying girl doesn't make money," is a common refrain from brothel owners.

We know only God can heal someone like Anju. But we also know it is our responsibility to give girls like Anju dignity, care, and respect while they face this terrible disease.

At the Home of Hope, Anju had grown close to the workers and other women who live there. She said they were closer to her than any sister could be. Day after day her friends gathered around her and prayed.

"Touch her body, dear Jesus," one friend said.

"Lift her up," prayed another. "Make her new; take away all the pain."

Anju was too weak to verbalize her prayers, but she whispered "Jesus!" over and over again. Her barely audible voice could not be heard over the chorus of petitions and praise emanating from her room.

Here, there was no threat that Anju would die alone on the streets. Her sisters and the staff members had guaranteed that. Hour after hour, a friend sat by her bed reading the Bible, praying and gently rubbing her arm. Workers brought her food and water. In all her life Anju had never known such care, mercy and love.

Within days of the prayer meeting, Anju -only 24 years old—passed into eternity. The staff and her roommates were saddened but they rejoiced in the knowledge she would never suffer at the hands of others again ... or from a merciless disease. Anju was now in the presence of Jesus.

These moments are the hardest, but also some of the most treasured. When we demonstrate the love of Christ to young women who have been violated and condemned, others in the community are attracted to that love and care, too.

THE SPREAD OF AIDS

AIDS is a one-way street to death. But when spiritual intervention is possible, that death gives way to eternal life. A young woman may have contracted the disease after a life of almost uninterrupted sorrow. But, having given that broken life to Christ, she moves on to a glorious future.

There are times when God divinely intervenes and defeats death. One girl came to Project Rescue and was healed of AIDS. We rejoice for such miracles. But in most cases the infected women are not healed.

"Here's my heartbreak," Devaraj once told us. "A group of girls with AIDS come to us and we do everything we can to help them. Only one gets healed and the others die. That poses a question that will never be answered this side of heaven."

Multitudes of women and girls are trafficked in India and around the world who are completely vulnerable to AIDS and every other sexually transmitted disease (STD). In India, in particular, it is difficult to pinpoint exactly how widespread the AIDS epidemic is. Statistics and data vary depending on what research is used. Some researchers estimate that there are nearly 6 million cases in the country. Another study claims India may have only 2 to 3 million cases. Bill Gates visited India several years ago to donate $100 million to fight AIDS. At the time, his organization's studies indicated India's AIDS cases could swell to 25 million by 2010. Regardless of the number of people infected, it is clear that it has reached epidemic proportions. And the vast majority of its victims are not getting the medical attention and care they need.

The AIDS crisis is spreading rapidly throughout India in large part because of sexual contact. According to medical experts, the hot spots for HIV infection—the highest rates of infection—are around the sites of religious pilgrimage. It is not coincidence that the major temple sites of India are the hottest HIV infection zones.

In December of 2005 *The New York Times* reported that India's highways were contributing to the spread of AIDS. "The national highways between New Delhi, Calcutta, Chennai, formerly Madras, and Mumbai [Bombay] run through at least six districts where HIV prevalence is above 2.5 percent. India's entry into the global economy over the past 15 years may also be furthering the spread of AIDS. With rising incomes, men have more money for sex; poor women see selling sex as their only access to the new prosperity. Cities are drawing more migrants and prostitutes, and Western influences are liberalizing Indian sexual mores."[4]

AIDS does not discriminate based on age or gender. To add to the crisis the public disapproves strongly of anyone who might become infected. In many ways having AIDS is like having leprosy. If children, particularly girls, get the disease they face stiff opposition and rejection.

According to a report aired on CBS, many doctors refuse to treat—or even touch—HIV-positive children. Some schools expel or segregate children because they or their parents are HIV-positive. In a society where females are already undervalued (they receive less food, education and medical care), contracting the HIV virus is an additional burden because of the scarce resources available to them.[5]

According to Doe Nair, head of a women's group that runs a children's home, almost all the girls at the government-funded home have been abandoned by their families after testing positive for HIV. "The premium for a male child is so high in Indian society that families are ready to spend on his medical treatment and care," Nair said.[6]

With the spread of AIDS, younger girls become direct targets of men carrying the disease. There is a myth widely accepted in Asia, Africa, and the Middle East that a person with HIV/AIDS or another STD can be cured if he has sex with a virgin. It is common to see wealthy businessmen from other countries come to India willing to pay top dollar so they can rape a little girl in a superstitious effort to rid themselves of a problem or disease.

It is believed that in India the migration of men to major cities for work also contributes to the epidemic. Typically, men are away from home and in the cities at their jobs for 11 months out of the year. There, they are without their wives, and many regularly visit the brothels. Then they go home for a month and often pass HIV to their wives.

A WORLD AT RISK

AIDS is a worldwide scourge placing the trafficked population at enormous risk. UNAIDS, the Joint United Nations Programme on HIV/AIDS, reported the following in 2006: "The 2005 Human Development Report identified AIDS as the factor inflicting the single greatest reversal in human development history (United Nations Development Programme, 2005). Between 1990 and 2003, many of the countries most severely affected by AIDS dropped sharply in the global ranking of countries on the Human Development Index. South Africa fell by 35 places, Zimbabwe by 23, Botswana by 21, Swaziland by 20, Kenya by 18, Zambia by 16 and Lesotho by 15. (The report ranked 135 countries across regions, using data from both 1990 and 2003.)"[7]

"The overall impact of AIDS on the global population has not yet reached its peak, and its demographic effects will likely be felt well into the second half of the 21st century. Current projections suggest that by 2015, in the 60 countries most affected by AIDS, the total population will be 115 million less than it would be in the absence of AIDS.[8]

"In Asia, a high proportion of new HIV infections are contracted during paid sex. In Viet Nam, HIV prevalence among female sex workers increased rapidly throughout the 1990s, from

0.06% in 1994 to 6% in 2002. In Indonesia, the rate of HIV infection among female sex workers is 3.1% nationally but varies significantly from region to region.

"In Jakarta, for example, it reached 6.4% in 2003 (MAP, 2005). In China, it is estimated that sex workers and their clients account for just less than 20% of the total number of people living with HIV (Ministry of Health, People's Republic of China/UNAIDS, 2005a)."[9]

AIDS is no longer a disease confined to developing countries. It is no longer a crisis confined to the inner city. AIDS is a global catastrophe, infecting every corner of the world.

ON THE GROUND

Her sweet singsong voice drifted out of the small hospital room. Curious, Devaraj entered the room to see who was singing in such a beautiful way.

When he entered the room, the little girl, sitting on a bed next to her baby brother, greeted him with an infectious smile, accented by her large brown eyes.

"What is your name?" Devaraj asked, stooping down to bed level.

The little girl stopped singing for a moment, then looked at him and said, "Shavanah," before continuing to sing.

Devaraj eyed the baby boy who was no older than 2 years of age. An IV tube ran to his tiny veins. Devaraj was certain he was HIV-positive and fighting for his life. He was weak and close to death. Shavanah seemed to know this too, but she wasn't about to give up on her little brother. After all, he was all she had left in the world.

"You don't have anything to worry about," sang Shavanah, who was not more than 4 years old. "I will take care of you; I won't let anyone harm you. You can depend on me. I am your sister, mommy and daddy. You don't have to worry about anything."

Shavanah stopped for a second, doted on her brother with her eyes, smiled at Devaraj, then began singing her song again. It was a song she had obviously made up, but the sincerity and love she conveyed with her simple words exposed an optimistic faith Devaraj could not ignore.

He left the room and went to find a nurse or doctor with whom to speak about Shavanah and her brother. During the brief meeting with a nurse he learned that Shavanah and her brother were recently orphaned, their mother had recently died of AIDS, and the little boy was HIV positive and not expected to live.

Like many children in India, Shavanah was on the fast track to adulthood. Despite her age she was being forced to act as the parent. Devaraj offered to take them in to our Project Rescue home where AIDS babies and children live.

Walking into the Bombay Teen Challenge AIDS home can jolt even the most distracted person back to the godly priorities of taking care of widows and orphans (James 1:27). When unsuspecting visitors enter the home, the children start singing to them. In Hindi they sing songs like "Open the eyes of my heart, Lord."

One day we heard them singing "Holy, holy, holy, Lord God Almighty …." Immediately, chills ran down our spines. Their voices were far from perfect … actually very reminiscent of a school choir where each child tries to outdo his or her neighbor. But their sincerity and admiration for the Lord is unrivaled.

Many of the children are orphaned and infected with HIV. The sad reality is that some of these children will die cruel deaths. Despite this they happily sing, "God has made us, He's made us who we are."

Among the children in the home are Shavanah and her little brother. Both children have blossomed on several fronts. Shavanah's little brother wanted a new name when he accepted Christ as his Savior. Now he is known as Peter. To see him is to see God's handiwork. Peter's health has been restored and he is a robust bundle of energy. Shavanah has continued to mature beyond her years—emotionally and spiritually. She loves to study the Bible and sing praise songs to Jesus.

The Bible commands us to care for orphans. Project Rescue takes the injunction of James 1:27 seriously. While we rejoice in the good news of lives transformed, such as Shavanah's and Peter's, we also realize, and must never forget, the countless other children who are victims of slavery, poverty and AIDs. This is no time to rest on one's laurels or to say, "We've done enough." To the contrary, it is the images of forsaken children that are embedded in our minds, and our love for Jesus, that push us toward the goal of rescuing more AIDS-orphans and children from the red-light districts of the world.

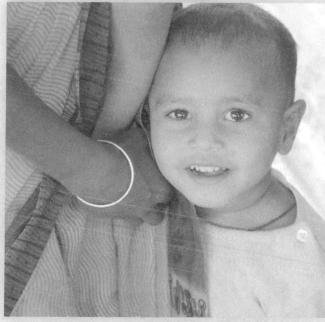

"Tears shed for self are tears of weakness, but tears shed for others are a sign of strength."[1]
—Billy Graham

CHAPTER SEVEN

A BIBLICAL MANDATE

The years of abuse in the brothel had taken their toll on 27-year-old Nikita. Cigarette burns. Contaminated food. And imprisonment in a dimly lit, insect-infested cubicle.

Nikita had been brought to Bombay with the promise of a good job. Instead she was forced into prostitution.

With each passing day she grew more numb and lifeless. She was losing her ability to feel anything, let alone respond to the sexual demands of her customers.

Suicide was growing more attractive.

One night, a dissatisfied customer with a thin mustache and thick arms drew back his hand and slapped Nikita's face.

Dazed, blood streamed from her nose.

The man cursed. "You're worthless," he said. "I want my money back!"

The apologetic madam rushed in. "I will get you

another girl," she said.

"No, I demand my money."

The madam shoved rupees into the man's chest and yelled at Nikita. "You're a disgrace to me."

Moments later, Nikita snapped. She stripped off her clothing and ran naked into the streets screaming uncontrollably.

No one wanted to come near her for fear Nikita would turn violent. The police were called.

One of the BTC workers thought quickly and wrapped a sheet around the trembling woman.

The worker prayed.

Instantly Nikita melted.

Tears followed.

Her brothel owner arrived on the scene with a string of insults. "I don't need you," he growled. "You're as good as dead."

When the police arrived, they released Nikita into the care of K.K. Devaraj.

Each day, for 10 months, the BTC staff prayed that God would heal Nikita of her emotional scars and the guilt that engulfed her. Counselors became accustomed to her outbursts, threats and physical attacks.

Some believed Nikita had lost her mind. Only a miracle could restore her to wholeness. Nevertheless they continued to pray and show her the love of Christ.

In time, smiles returned to Nikita's face. And the angry, hateful words that littered her counseling sessions disappeared. She began to attend church services and could be seen trying to sing along.

One day, during a counseling session, Nikita asked if she could pray.

"Yes, please pray," the worker said.

Nikita's voice was unusually soft and soothing.

"Dear Jesus, I love You. Please help me," she prayed, with tears forming in her eyes. "I need Your help."

That was her breakthrough.

Eighteen months later a beautifully dressed, vibrant woman walked onto a platform as she was honored for her completion of a discipleship training program. God had brought a miraculous spiritual, emotional and physical healing.

OUR DUTY

Jewish social activist Michael Horowitz documents that, historically, evangelical Christians have risked everything to care for the most vulnerable victims of injustice and poverty. Christ's followers are compelled to respond to tragedies like sex-slave trafficking because of our commitment to serve Jesus by serving the weak, disadvantaged and exploited. We believe in the power of the gospel to transform the lives of girls like Nikita. We believe it is our duty, based on the Word of God, to proclaim the value of women and the girl children.[2]

Every human life is created by God and stamped with His image (Genesis 1:27). Lives have been tarnished by sin, but can be restored by the redemptive work of Jesus Christ and God's love (2 Corinthians 5:17; Galatians 3:26). Each person is unique in God's creation, endowed with God-given gifts and a God-ordained purpose. As such, each man, woman and child is equally deserving of love, respect and dignity (Galatians 3:28,29).

Woman is a creation of God (Genesis 1:27), lovingly made in His likeness. She was created as an equal partner and helper for man, to serve God alongside him (Genesis 2:18). God blessed the woman He created and gave her authority with man over the other life forms He had fashioned (Genesis 1:28-30).

The value God places on His female creation is revealed in the roles He ordained them to fill in accomplishing His eternal purposes at pivotal moments in the history of His people. Miriam, the sister of Moses and Aaron, was called by God as a prophetess and leader during the Israelites' exodus from Egypt (Exodus 15:20,21). Deborah, a prophetess and wife of Lappidoth, was chosen by God to lead the Israelites into battle against the Canaanites (Judges 4). Ruth, a Moabite woman, established herself in Israel's history by becoming an ancestress of King David (Ruth 4:18-22) and Jesus Christ (Matthew 1:1,5). The Jewess Esther was sovereignly ordained by God to become queen in a land of exile in order to deliver His people from destruction (Esther 4:14).

The record of the New Testament is just as illuminating in the ways women were used as instruments for God's purposes in the life and ministry of His Son, Jesus. God's favor on young Mary was dramatically pronounced by an angel who said she would give birth to the incarnate Son of God (Luke 1:30,31). After His birth, the elderly prophetess Anna attended the infant Jesus' presentation at the temple and announced the significance of His birth to those who were looking for the redemption of Jerusalem (Luke 2:36-38).

During the terrifying hours of Jesus' crucifixion, when the earth shook in agony, Mary Magdalene, Mary the mother of James and Joseph, and the mother of the sons of Zebedee faithfully attended to their dying Lord (Matthew 27:55,56). After Jesus' death, women disciples came to His burial place and discovered that He had risen from the dead (Luke 23:55,56; 24:1-6). Theirs was the joy of first announcing the message of Jesus' resurrection that would forever change the course of history.

JESUS VALUED WOMEN

The manner by which Jesus treated women

during His life on earth also reveals the value He placed on them. As He traveled with His disciples through Samaria, Jesus demonstrated His esteem for a Samaritan woman at the well by engaging her in conversation and revealing His identity as the Messiah (John 4:26). Jesus displayed respect and concern for women in a culture that frequently relegated them to secondary, even menial, status. His relationship with Mary and Martha is reflected in His concern for them at the time of their brother's death (John 11). The way in which the sisters freely related their frustrations and fears to Jesus spoke to the level of friendship that He shared with them. This was the Mary who anointed Jesus' feet with expensive perfume and wiped His feet with her hair (John 12:1-3). On that occasion when Judas publicly objected to her extravagant deed, Jesus publicly defended Mary's act of devotion (John 12:7).

Another meaningful glimpse of Jesus' awareness and concern for women is provided in Luke 13:10-17. While teaching in a synagogue, the Master Teacher caught sight of a woman who had been crippled for 18 years. Calling her to himself, He laid His hands on her and healed her—to the indignation of those watching. Rebuking His critics for their hypocrisy, Jesus honored the rejoicing woman with a reminder that she was "a daughter of Abraham," deserving of the freedom from bondage that He had bestowed.

In Luke 8, both a young girl who had died
and an older woman with a 12-year history of
bleeding are the objects of Jesus' compassion.
While on His way to pray over Jairus' young
daughter, Jesus sensed that healing had come
to someone in the crowd who touched Him.
Knowing who she was, He called the woman
with an issue of blood out of the crowd and
commended her great faith (Luke 8:47,48).

Even a woman who was about to be stoned by
religious leaders was treated with love and respect
by the Son of God. The apostle John records the
dramatic scene where a woman caught in the act
of adultery was physically forced before Jesus
by the accusing Pharisees (John 8:1-11). When
questioned about what this sinful woman's fate
should be, Jesus did not add to her humiliation.
Instead He addressed her directly, acknowledging
her sin without condemning her. He offered
her a future free from the bondage of sin. By
His compassionate actions toward women, and
His willingness to include them in His life and
ministry, Jesus reinforced that women were
created as intended recipients of God's love and
redemptive work.

After Jesus' death and resurrection, it was
left to His disciples to carry on His work,
empowered by the Holy Spirit (Acts 1:15; 2:4).
Women, along with men, were called, gifted and
empowered by God for diverse ministries within

the Early Church. Among the women named and commended for their active roles were: Priscilla, teacher and co-worker with the apostle Paul (Romans 16:3; Acts 18:23-28) and Phoebe, a deaconess (Romans 16:1,2). Many commentators believe that Junia, an apostle commended in Romans 16:7, was a woman. Throughout the apostle Paul's writings, women are commended for their help in the ministries of the fledging church (Romans 16:1-12). Women were not only created by God and recipients of Christ's redemption, but an integral part of the Spirit-empowered ministries of the body of Christ.

If we believe in the value of every human life, including the unique and vital role God ordained for women, we have no choice but to fight for the victims of the sex-slave industry. Project Rescue was raised up to restore to women the hope and dignity that the enemy has stolen from them.

THE GREAT COMMISSION

Jesus' last recorded instructions to His disciples in the Gospels are found in Matthew 28:18-20: "All authority in heaven and on earth has been given to me. Therefore go and make disciples of all nations, baptizing them in the name of the Father and of the Son and of the Holy Spirit, and teaching them to obey everything I have

commanded you." All nations includes men,
women and children of every people group,
language, caste, and class, regardless of economic,
social and religious categories. It includes millions
of exploited women and children caught in the
horrendous evil of sexual slavery. The Great
Commission compels us to go, preach and work
to bring new life to victims through Jesus Christ
wherever they are, whatever their condition. The
life-changing promise that if any man or woman
be "in Christ" (in faith relationship to Him)
they are a new creation applies not only to the
educated woman in a corporate boardroom or the
housewife living in suburbia. The promise also
pertains to the prostituted teenager dying of AIDS
in a brothel in Bombay, India.

But how does one confront the dark and
dangerous face of evil called sexual trafficking and
see victims like Nikita supernaturally changed?
The answer is found in God's Word, where it
says He works through His people. He gives us
strategies, courage, power, ideas and resources
to be used for His glory, to reach out to women
and girls in need. He desires to rescue and restore
them more than we do. He is simply looking for
people who are willing to do their part, to raise
their hands and say, "Lord, show me what I can
do."

Jesus said, "The Spirit of the Lord is on me,
because he has anointed me to preach good news

to the poor. He has sent me to proclaim freedom for the prisoners and recovery of sight for the blind, to release the oppressed, to proclaim the year of the Lord's favor"(Luke 4:18,19). Likewise He is calling on us to work for the freedom and release of brutalized women and children around the world in the power of His Spirit. He is calling us to work to bring physical, spiritual and relational healing.

MEETING NEEDS

By both His recorded words and His actions, Jesus Christ demonstrated that He came to earth to bring healing and new life to the whole person—body, soul and spirit. While proclaiming himself the bread of life through whom all who believe have eternal life (John 6:48-51), the Son of God tangibly demonstrated His concern for the physical, emotional, mental and relational well-being of people.

The Gospels are filled with stories of Jesus meeting the physical needs of men, women and children. As Jesus was leaving Jericho, for example, He encountered two blind men by the side of the road. He responded to their cries for help and miraculously gave them sight (Matthew 20:29-34).

Jesus also met spiritual needs. In Mark 9:17-27,

an anguished father brought his son to Jesus. The
boy was controlled by evil spirits and susceptible
to violent seizures. Jesus confronted the demonic
power and, instantly, the boy experienced spiritual
freedom. When the woman who was caught in the
act of adultery and was about to be stoned for her
sin was brought to Him, Jesus broke all religious
and cultural norms by offering her forgiveness and
a new life without sin (John 8:1-11).

The woman Jesus met at the well in Samaria
was engaged in a series of sexual relationships
that revealed relational failure, spiritual death
and social alienation. Rather than devaluating her
because of her failures, Jesus spoke into her life
with the truth of who He is as the Messiah. The
woman excitedly announced her life-changing
encounter with the Son of God (John 4:1-26).

Relational healing was also important to Jesus.
In Luke 15, He shared the story of a loving father
who grieves over his son who left home on a
journey of self-destruction. When the son realized
he was wasting his life and his father's resources,
he returned home with a repentant heart. The
father ran to welcome his lost son, full of
forgiveness and hope of restoration. The forgiving,
restoring, loving father is a powerful image for
broken humanity, people everywhere who have
lost relationship with their Heavenly Father. In
Matthew 22:37, Jesus declared that the greatest
commandment is: "Love the Lord your God with

all your heart and with all your soul and with all
your mind." This ultimate purpose for all men,
women and children can only be attained when
they have been touched by the Son of God's loving
power in every dimension of their lives.

A JOURNEY

It is heart-wrenching, however, to pray with
women in sexual bondage for God's healing
and deliverance and then watch them return to
the brothel. But we have learned that spiritual
and physical freedom is often a journey, much
like the Exodus of the Israelites from slavery in
Egypt. Often it is a trek, rather than an instant
translation. Sometimes spiritual freedom comes
before physical freedom can be obtained; in other
cases, physical freedom is negotiated first, and
spiritual, emotional, and mental freedom follow
as victims experience Christ's love and healing in
a Home of Hope. No matter the timing or order
of events, Jesus is ultimately the only One who
can, and does, bring total freedom and new life
to those in bondage. Time and again, we have
seen Him honor His Word. We have seen His love
reach into dark, depraved places and transform
the lives of enslaved women.

Trafficking is not a new phenomenon. The Bible
contains many references to slavery, prejudice

and abuse. Joseph, in Genesis 37:13-28, was sold
into slavery by his brothers. The Israelites were
in bondage to the Egyptians in Genesis 46 and
47. Yet, time and again, God worked through
circumstances and used men and women to bring
about justice. Joseph was promoted to an office
of great influence. The Israelites were also set free
from slavery.

When Jesus came 2,000 years ago, He came
to proclaim freedom for the oppressed and to
set the captive free. He came to liberate us from
the consequences of sin so we could inherit
eternal life. And, as followers of Christ, we are
commanded to work with Him to abolish all
forms of slavery and injustice.

[I've seen] "firsthand the vulnerabilities created by war, depression and economic displacement. Under such conditions, it is easy to see how women and children are the most exposed and vulnerable to exploitation."[1]

—*Angelina Jolie*

CHAPTER EIGHT

INTERVENTION, RESTORATION, PREVENTION

The power of Jesus' transforming touch was evident in Nalini's eyes. When she started coming to our church services she looked like a woman spent. She was downcast, angry and calloused. Years of suffering at the hands of men added onto years of inflicting brutality on other women had robbed Nalini of any joy or peace.

"How long have you been in prostitution?" one of our workers asked.

Nalini weighed the question, then said, "I used to be a prostitute; now I'm a madam."

We wondered if she thought because she was a madam she wouldn't be welcome. After all, the madams are typically demanding of the girls. They play a crucial role in the confinement and discipline of those they prostitute. The relationship is seldom a peaceful one.

"We welcome you in the name of the Lord," said the worker. "Come and worship with us."

Nalini stayed for the church service that day. A few days later she attended another service. The pattern continued and eventually she committed her life to Jesus Christ.

Suddenly there was a vibrant look about her. Hope filled her eyes and a generous smile creased her lips.

"I have so much peace and joy," she exclaimed. "God is great!"

We rejoiced with Nalini. For months she came to church, then returned afterward to manage her brothel. This may be difficult for a Western Christian to understand. But in Bombay we cannot demand that a woman leave the brothel, though we do everything possible to help her gain her freedom.

Even with the madams, who have more power and less risk should they leave the brothel, it is a delicate situation for them to abandon their only means of making a living. For such women, leaving the brothel is a frightening proposition. Finding honorable work is next to impossible. They could easily end up back in the brothel in prostitution ... or out on the streets penniless.

One day Nalini came into church with tears streaking her face. Her chest heaved with sobs and the workers feared something awful had happened to her.

"What is wrong, Nalini?"

"I can't do this anymore. I cannot keep the girls."

The Project Rescue worker nodded. "I understand. Jesus understands."

"I feel very bad for being a madam," admitted Nalini behind a waterfall of tears.

"Tell us how we can help you."

The madam wiped her eyes. "I am releasing all of my girls and want you to use my brothel as a prayer hall."

The worker smiled. "I will tell Uncle Devaraj of your offer. He will be very pleased. God will honor you."

Thanks to Nalini, today in the heart of the red-light district is a prayer hall that also acts as medical clinic, night-care facility and distribution point of food and clothing.

Nalini's story illustrates the importance of our three-pronged approach to ministry: intervention, restoration, and prevention.

INTERVENTION

The first Project Rescue Home of Hope was opened to be a place of safety, healing and compassionate care. It has grown into a multidimensional rescue ministry for trafficking victims and their children. More than 1,000 victimized women and girls in India and Nepal have been helped. Though the ministry has grown to 11 Homes of Hope in nine Southern Asian cities—including Bombay, Kolkata, Pune, Nagpur, and Katmandu—it remains a ministry of hope and recovery.

Intervention includes efforts to physically rescue women and girls from sexual slavery. Doing so is a complex, drawn-out process that basically encompasses three main elements:

1. We negotiate the release of enslaved women and girls from brothels.

2. We accept into Homes of Hope trafficking victims who've been rescued during police raids.

3. We intervene to get children of prostituted women out of the brothels during work hours and into Project Rescue Night-Care Centers.

When a girl's release is negotiated from the brothels people assume money is involved. During the first year of Project Rescue's existence, Bombay Teen Challenge workers paid some of the girl's "debts" to the brothel owners in order to attain their release. However, it quickly became apparent that this strategy put money back into the hands of organized crime members and procurers to obtain other young sex slaves. As a result, Project Rescue workers now exhaust every means possible in the negotiation process without offering payment. Working relationships

have been established with police, brothel
owners, madams and even the girls who work
in the red-light district. These relationships have
been invaluable to ministry and our quest to get
girls released. Devaraj and other Project Rescue
workers have become known for their genuine
compassion for everyone in the district and their
willingness to demonstrate Christ's love in tangible
ways.

As Project Rescue has grown and proven itself
to be a credible Christian organization in India,
police in several cities now contact Home of
Hope administrators when a trafficking raid is
conducted and girls are taken into custody.

State-run aftercare for victims rescued in police
raids is minimal. Project Rescue intervenes by
offering quality aftercare facilities that give
women a safe place to recover. The Project Rescue
Home of Hope in Pune, India, is a pilot project in
partnership with the government. The agreement
allows girls to be sent to the Pune Project Rescue
Home of Hope for intervention and restoration.
If this collaboration is successful, there will be
opportunities for expansion.

Intervention also takes place through "night-
care centers" in Bombay, Nagpur and Kolkata.
Buildings adjacent to the red-light districts provide
safe places for the children of enslaved women.
The centers are especially critical to vulnerable
children, getting them out of their mother's room

when she is servicing customers. Like a traditional day-care facility, the Project Rescue night-care centers offer nourishing food, tutoring, and a place children can sleep. They also learn about God's love for them and His power to change their circumstances.

RESTORATION

The Project Rescue restoration strategy addresses the physical, emotional, spiritual and educational needs of rescued women and girls as they are discipled. Restoration includes the following components offered at each Home of Hope functioning as a caring Christian community:

- General medical care
- Counseling for the trauma of abuse and exploitation
- Basic literacy training
- Christian discipleship
- Vocational training leading to financial independence
- Hospice care for women dying of AIDS in Katmandu, Nepal, and Bombay.

Four of the 11 Project Rescue Homes of Hope in Southern Asia are also focused on ministry to the children of prostituted women. In both Kolkata and Nagpur—as in Bombay—women enslaved in the red-light district have been willing to relinquish their daughters so they can escape the horrors of the brothels. Trust has been built between Project Rescue care-givers and the mothers as they've watched their daughters receive care. As a result, mothers enslaved in the brothels have gained the courage to request help and start their own journey toward physical, spiritual and emotional healing.

A high percentage of women entrapped in sexual slavery in Bombay have been trafficked from poverty-stricken villages in Nepal. For those who desire to return home to Nepal, the ministry aids in repatriation and provides aftercare at the Home of Hope in Katmandu, Nepal. If the women desire to reconnect with their families, Project Rescue workers facilitate that process.

However, since an increasing percentage of the women being rescued are HIV positive or already suffering from AIDS, they are not often welcomed back by their families or communities in Nepal. In such tragic cases, the Home of Hope staff and other rescued women in the program become their new family. They surround their "sisters" in Christ with love, dignity and support as they live their final days.

Some of the most effective workers in Project Rescue are former madams. Rescued from the brothels themselves, they courageously go into the district and work to bring other enslaved women out of bondage and into a new and fulfilling life in Christ. One former madam was honored as a goddess during religious festivals because of her demonic power. Upon being transformed by Christ's love, she began leading other women out of sexual slavery and nurturing them in their journey of faith.

PREVENTION

Potential tragedies are best addressed by prevention. Saving girls before they endure hardship is one of the most satisfying aspects of Project Rescue. Together Project Rescue workers, supporters and leaders have kept countless girls out of the brothels. Doing so requires the implementation of pre-emptive measures. Following is our basic strategy:

- Provide safe houses—Homes of Hope—for daughters of prostituted women before they are forced into sexual slavery themselves.
- Conduct AIDS and sex trafficking awareness projects in the high-risk areas of Western Nepal and North India.
- Intervene in the sale of girls and women to traffickers.
- Implement initiatives at Nepal/India border crossings.

Homes of Hope, established for daughters of

prostituted women, directly save them from a
life of sexual slavery in the brothels. Daughters
are generally placed in the Homes of Hope at the
mother's request or by a madam when the child's
mother dies. Ongoing contact between the mother
and child is encouraged by the staff. The children
are encouraged to pray regularly for their mothers
who are still enslaved. Meanwhile, little girls who
were once destined for sexual exploitation are
loved, cared for in a safe place, and educated to
become the women God created them to be.

Prevention also occurs in the Western areas of
the nation of Nepal, as well as Northern India.
Procurers who traffic Nepali girls into Indian
brothels tend to go to the same poverty-stricken
areas to convince families to sell their daughters.
Project Rescue, in partnership with Nepali
Assemblies of God churches, has conducted
community awareness projects to educate families
in high-risk areas.

Communities of Hope in Western Nepal were
established as bases for adult awareness, basic
literacy training for girl children, medical clinics,
and spiritual outreach in the local community.
Similar communities need to be established
throughout the world where human-trafficking
exists.

As the ministry of Project Rescue has become
known, another aspect of prevention has begun to
take shape. On a number of occasions, ministry

personnel have been confidentially notified by concerned villagers that a family is in the process of negotiating the sale of a daughter to traffickers. Staff personnel have been able to intervene and prevent the sale of a number of young girls into sexual slavery by offering financial help to the impoverished parents and arranging to place their daughter in a Christian home or orphanage.

Project Rescue's three-pronged approach comes from the Word of God. Throughout the Bible we see that God's way is restoration, intervention and prevention. He heals people physically and emotionally. He intervenes in their lives when they are on the road to destruction. And He gives them a roadmap that will prevent them from experiencing less than God's best for their lives.

"There are people in the world so hungry, that God cannot appear to them except in the form of bread."[1]

—*Mahatma Gandhi*

CHAPTER NINE

A PLAN OF ACTION

At 16 years of age Ayushi had suffered more than four years of rape, abuse and neglect. The toll on her had been exacting and compounded with a deep feeling of depression and thoughts of suicide. Sometimes when she had a free moment she escaped to the rooftop of her brothel and stood at the roof's edge. As she stared down at the city's steady hum of activity, she contemplated jumping. But each time she found the nerve to go through with it, one of her madams appeared and pulled her to safety.

"You cannot deny your karma," scolded the madam, slapping Ayushi across the face. "This is your life. Accept it."

Ayushi's misery grew each night as men descended on Falkland Road, leering at the brothel like demons searching for someone to possess. As the night's first customer entered her room every fiber of her being screamed for her to run to safety. But she was trained to submit to his demands.

It seemed as if the man, like so many before him, had wrenched a small part of her soul away.

Enduring repeated violations, Ayushi stared into a future of endless nights just like this one. She decided that nothing but death could release her from her grim existence. The following day she scrounged for food while again entertaining thoughts of suicide. She wept quietly and spent much of the day lying on her bed. As night fell she stifled her sobs and pulled at her hair.

"If this behavior persists I'll beat her," threatened one of Ayushi's madams, just outside her door.

Ayushi heard the woman's words, but she no longer cared. Maybe a good beating would be her way out … her way to death. As the other girls prepared for the night, Ayushi ran out of her room, down the hallway and past the madams. They grabbed at her arms and cursed and threatened her, but she wriggled out of their grasp and dashed into the street.

Ayushi's eyes flitted in search of a fast-moving vehicle to put her out of her misery. Lost in the maze of streets, she collapsed into a sobbing heap on the side of the road. Eventually the madams found her and dragged her ruthlessly back to the brothel.

Ayushi was beaten mercilessly and shoved into a filthy room. The thick metal door slammed behind her and the padlock snapped shut.

"You can come out when you're ready to work," the madam spat.

Days later, Ayushi was allowed to return to her stall. Her listless eyes and lifeless body were grim physical evidence that her spirit and will had been broken once and for all.

When the brothel owner saw her vacant stare he was displeased. His once-prized investment was virtually useless. He now could only ponder the value of the bed she was occupying. "Throw her out into the street," he demanded. In a strange act of apparent kindness, the madams begged him to let her stay. But their reasons for doing so had little to do with compassion ... and everything to do with money.

"She is the most beautiful of all the girls," they said. "We must call K.K. Devaraj. Maybe he can help her."

The brothel owner contemplated the madams' recommendation.

"I will call him," he said.

Devaraj had learned that to survive as a minister on Falkland Road he had to build an intricate relational network that would extend from exploited girls to brothel owners all the way to the police commissioner's office. On the surface, the building of relationships with such men would appear treacherous. But Devaraj knew that doing so would build goodwill and position him to rescue more girls and share his faith in Christ.

Less than an hour after receiving the call from the brothel owner, Devaraj found himself sitting at the bedside of the young woman. He prayed for her and asked God to heal her body, soul and mind.

"We must take her to a hospital," he said, eyeing the brothel owner. "She needs medical attention."

The brothel owner looked down on Ayushi and considered Devaraj's request. "Would you like to purchase her from me?"

"No," Devaraj said. "I'm here to help her, not own her."

The owner weighed his options.

"Then do as you wish with her," he said with a wave of his hand. "I've lost my use for her. She is yours."

Devaraj and his team hastily led the young woman out of the brothel and to the hospital.

Weeks later, when Ayushi was released from the hospital, Devaraj's team admitted her to a Home of Hope. There, she accepted Christ as her Lord and Savior. Her wish had come true. Death had come to her old life and a new life had begun.

NEGOTIATING FREEDOM

In Bombay, freedom for the girls does not come without a price. From the moment they arrive at the brothels, they are indebted to their owners for such large sums of money it will literally take years—if not a lifetime—to pay down the debt. For many girls, disease and death come long before their so-called debts are settled.

Because of the compassionate work of Devaraj and his team on Falkland Road, they have earned the trust of the community. Some brothel owners have expressed their gratitude by forgiving girls' debts and turning them over to BTC-Project Rescue. They have taken notice of the free medical checkups, food give-aways and concern for the children. As Proverbs 18:16 says, "A gift opens the way for the giver."

The people of Falkland Road have seen that we are not there to exploit them, but rather to help them. Devaraj has become recognized in the community as a man of God. The police and politicians have been willing to help him free a girl in certain circumstances.

"There is a young girl in this brothel," Devaraj might say to a police officer. "She is a follower of Jesus and one day we are hoping and praying that she will be free."

"I will talk to her owner and see what I can do," the officer often responds.

And, occasionally, the Lord will convict the corrupt heart of a brothel owner and prompt him to let a girl go free.

WILL YOU FORGET?

In 1997 we toured Falkland Road with Devaraj and our hearts were broken. We felt a sense of hopelessness, knowing that literally thousands of little girls were being brutalized and exploited.

Something rose up in our souls. It was as if God was interrogating us: *Who will be the father of these little ones? Will you simply forget them? What will you allow Me to do through you?*

As we prayed with Devaraj, we knew we had to help the girls find a way out of the brothels. We had to offer an alternative to the miserable lives they led. That is when we started shedding light on the problem and asking believers around the world to partner with Project Rescue to establish Homes of Hope and shelters for at-risk children.

Since then, many prostituted women and their children have made Jesus their Lord and Savior. They have been rescued from the brothels and received training and an education. And they've been reunited with their families. Project Rescue continues to grow, which means more women and children can experience wholeness and find purpose in their lives.

In *Bombay, India*, there is a Teen Challenge Center, HIV clinic and a Home of Hope women's shelter. Three additional homes were built for the children of prostituted women, where they learn computer skills, math, reading and more. A night-care shelter was also established for the babies so they could escape the horrors of the brothels. In addition, a prayer hall was opened in a former brothel.

In *Ashagram, India*, a 48-acre farm was developed, which serves as a center for restoration and vocational training. There, the women reside in four homes and receive training in dress and jewelry making, embroidery and leather craft.

In *Katmandu, Nepal*, Home of Hope and Community of Hope centers have been established to help integrate women into the community and minister to them. Vocational training and counseling are also made available to women attempting to put their lives back together. Income producing projects—such as making purses, shawls and journals that can be sold—have also assisted women in their journey to recovery and meaning.

In *Nepalgunj, Nepal*, a number of programs have been established to help victimized women recapture their dignity and set a course for a better life: vocational training, counseling, children's education, prayer groups, nutrition and hygiene care, and more.

In *Kolkata, India*, the children's home is a residential facility for girls at high risk for sexual abuse and HIV. An evening care center provides a safe learning environment for children living in the streets or in the brothels. A vocational training initiative is also in place for women who want to learn a trade and come out of prostitution.

In *Madras, India,* the Home of Hope affords the girls opportunity to attend school and grow in their love for God. Working in partnership with New Life Assembly of God Church, which has 35,000 parishioners, Project Rescue's Home of Hope is giving exploited girls and those at risk a new beginning.

In *Pune, India,* the Project Rescue Home of Hope offers a safe place to teenage girls rescued from the brothels during government raids. The girls receive an education, food, clothing and biblical instruction.

HOMES OF HOPE

When a girl arrives at a Home of Hope, she is encouraged to talk about her fears, anger, hatred, and other emotions. Doing so is a fast track to healing.

We also encourage them to choose a birthday and a new name. Many of the girls do not know how old they are or when they were born. We allow them to choose their birthday. Many select the day they were water baptized. Such a simple act can mean so much to a person trying to pick up the pieces of a shattered life.

The Homes of Hope allow girls and women to

live in a holistic environment that caters to their needs. We strive to provide biblical values so they can safely reintegrate with society. We educate them, give them job skills, take them to church and prepare them for everyday life.

For years many of the women have been forced to use their bodies to *make* money. We teach them to use acquired skills to *earn* money. Upon leaving, many women are able to generate income and support themselves by making and selling hand-made products.

Seventeen-year old Pabita came to the Katmandu Home of Hope in Nepal after being rescued from the brothels by police officers in India. Her story is similar to that of many young women in India and Nepal. Her mother was an alcoholic who beat Pabita day after day. When Pabita was 15 she couldn't take it anymore, so she ran away.

A woman in the village befriended her and invited her to stay in her home. It was a trap. After several days the woman drugged Pabita and put her on a train to Bombay, where she found herself working in a brothel. The girl was required to service countless men, day after day.

Miraculously, after eight months, she was freed from the brothel by police and sent back to Nepal. But the beatings at the hands of her mother escalated. So, Pabita fled to the Home of Hope.

After a year of living in a safe and secure environment and seeing the unconditional love of God demonstrated toward her, Pabita experienced spiritual and emotional healing. Today she knows Jesus as her Savior and for the first time has hope for a future. Every day she attends classes and has aspirations of becoming a nurse.

"Commit yourself to the noble struggle for human rights. You will make a greater person of yourself ... and a finer world to live in."

"Someone must have sense enough and religion enough to cut off the chain of hate and evil, and this can only be done through love."[1]

—Martin Luther King, Jr.

CHAPTER TEN

A GLOBAL STRATEGY

Joi had been prostituted since she was 11. But she wanted a better life for her 18-year-old daughter, Maya. She paid to have Maya stay at a hostel, rather than have her live in the brothel. But as Joi began to age and the wrinkles on her face became more pronounced, customers weren't as interested in her services. Money grew short and her madam became increasingly demanding.

"Joi, you must make money or you will be put out," the madam said.

"I am giving you everything," Joi replied.

"It's not enough," the madam snapped.

"What can I do?"

The madam was quick with her answer. "Bring us Maya. Let her take your place. She is young. Her skin is smooth. Men no longer want you."

"My daughter?"

"Yes, we will pay you."

"Not my daughter. I will try harder," Joi said.

"No matter what you do, Maya will become a prostitute. The gods have spoken. It is your family's place," the madam said.

Joi closed her eyes in agony. "How much will you give for her?"

"Bring her and we will see what she can earn," the madam said.

Joi summoned her daughter, unaware that Maya had been abused and raped by men in the hostel since she was a small child. But now none of that mattered to Joi. To live, she had no choice but to sell Maya into slavery.

For several years, Maya endured the pain of her mother's betrayal and the brutalization of men who didn't know her name. Finally, one day she could take no more; she escaped the brothel and found her way to the Home of Hope.

When Rebecca, our oldest daughter, met Maya, she found the young woman so emotionally scarred that she was blank-faced and unresponsive. Rebecca encouraged her to write about her feelings and fears. She wrote about her attempt to run away from the brothel, and how the owner threatened to kill her. She wrote about her desire to end her life. As Maya read to Rebecca from her journal, she began to weep.

Rebecca wrapped her arms around the young woman and let her cry until there were no more tears.

"Auntie Rebecca, when will I stop remembering?" she asked.

Rebecca replied, "You will always remember, but in time it won't hurt as much. Keep giving your pain to Jesus and ask Him to help you forgive those who have hurt you."

Maya shook her head, "Okay."

Weeks later, Maya agreed to tell her story through an interpretive dance. She moved with such grace and emotion, like one who had studied ballet in New York City.

All the girls applauded.

Maya cracked a smile and her deadened eyes came to life.

"Auntie Rebecca," Maya said. "I want you to know that before I was always crying on the inside, but now I'm smiling on the inside, too."

Rebecca again embraced the young woman, saying, "We love you. Jesus loves you. You are safe now. Never again will you have that life. It is part of your past, but it is no longer your future."

Like all the women rescued from the red-light district, Maya was encouraged to claim Ezekiel 36:25-27 as her own: "I will sprinkle clean water on you, and you will be clean; I will cleanse you from all your impurities and from all your idols. I will give you a new heart and put a new spirit in you; I will remove from you your heart of stone and give you a heart of flesh. And I will put my Spirit in you."

Sometime later, Maya said with a wide grin, "Auntie, I have found one more Scripture for me in Isaiah 54:4: 'Do not be afraid; you will not suffer shame. Do not fear disgrace; you will not be humiliated. You will forget the shame of your youth.'"

Because of Jesus' healing touch, Maya had come a long ways from the timid, blank-faced girl Rebecca had met weeks earlier. Maya now believed Jesus had given her a future.

GOD OF CONVERGENCE

We know that God founded Project Rescue. We merely have the privilege of serving Him to accomplish a work that is dear to His heart. He loves the exploited women and their children. He longs to liberate them. For that reason He has brought a team of workers and friends together to accomplish the task. Just as God called us and K.K. Devaraj to Project Rescue, He has spoken to Rebecca, Doug and Ramona Jacobs, Ambika Pandey, Mathew and Suhasini Daniel, Andy and Nancy Ratz and others. He has transformed the lives of young women enslaved in prostitution and molded them into effective ministry workers. He has called young people from Bible schools and universities to devote their lives to helping Project Rescue minister to the victims of the sex-slave industry. God has given us the favor of spiritual leaders like Thomas E. Trask, John Bueno, Jerry Parsley and Omar Beiler. He has given Project Rescue financial partners like First Assembly in North Little Rock, Arkansas; James River Assembly in Ozark, Missouri; Women's Ministries groups; Kay Burnett; Nancy Koetitz and others. We serve a God of convergence. He brings the right people and resources together to accomplish His tasks at the right time.

THE ENGINEER

Initially some might have wondered how an engineer with no ministerial training could become the vanguard of the struggle against child prostitution in Bombay. But we have all seen God's hand on the life of K.K. Devaraj. As a child, Devaraj frequented the temples and prayed to the gods. He took a position in Iran, working in the oil fields. While there, he was invited to attend a house church, where he was befriended by Christians. He was struck by their love and compassion and eventually surrendered his life to Christ. He moved to Lebanon, where he met Jim and Eloise Neely, who were working with the Teen Challenge center. God began to give Devaraj a burden for young men in bondage to drugs and alcohol.

Devaraj had no intention of returning to India, but God led him to enroll at Southern Asia Bible College at Bangalore. While attending college, he took part in a conference in Bombay and walked alone through the city. He sensed God speaking to him to begin a Teen Challenge outreach in Bombay. A short time later, with a Bible degree and no money, Devaraj boarded a train in Bangalore headed for Bombay. He launched the Teen Challenge work by going to the streets and sharing Christ with young men with addictions. He also witnessed to taxi drivers and shop owners. Regardless of the place people were at in life, he wanted to tell them about Jesus.

When Devaraj saw the living conditions of the brothels and how women and children were being treated, he wanted to do everything possible to help them. That was the beginning of Project Rescue and its partnership with BTC.

The United States Congress, wanting to curtail the sex exploitation of young girls and women, invited Devaraj to testify at a hearing in July 2004. Following is his testimony:

Children are the most vulnerable group in Mumbai [Bombay] and in need of the greatest social care. On account of their vulnerability and dependence they are exploited, ill-treated and directed into undesirable channels by anti-social elements in the city. It is plain for any visitor to Mumbai to see the gross violation of

the rights of children. In Mumbai, children are
denied the right to be born or exist, deprived
of family, deprived of opportunity and are
exploited and abused in appalling ways.

India signed the U.N. Convention on the
Rights of the Child in 1990. This implies an
obligation on the part of the Government of
India and its States to safeguard all children
from neglect, sexual exploitation and abuse
and to ensure their right to a family and
education. Among India's own laws, the
Children's Act of 1960 states that children are
the most vulnerable group in any population
and are in need of the greatest social care, the
State having the duty to protect them.

In 1986, the Indian Parliament enacted
the Juvenile Justice Act to provide for care,
protection, treatment, development and
rehabilitation of neglected or delinquent
juveniles. This Act was consolidated in 2000.

Despite the above laws, the reality is a stark
contrast.

There are observation (remand) homes
run by the State Government for children in
conflict with the law.

However, the children sent to these homes
are not necessarily in conflict with the law.
For example, children rescued from child
labor or brothels and the children of criminals
and prostituted women are also sent to these

homes. Although they are supposed to be kept in the observation homes for just 15 days, they often languish there for much longer periods of time, sometimes for years at a stretch.

Currently, the official figures are 2,500-3,000 children in observation homes in Mumbai city. In our experience, however, we've found that these homes are usually overcrowded and the number could be much higher.

From the observation homes, the children are sent on to various homes for juvenile delinquents, which are also run by the State Government. In some cases the children are sent to NGOs (non-government organizations).

The ideal home should have, at the very least, a well-regulated daily routine that should provide for a disciplined life, physical exercise, education, vocational training, recreation, moral education and group/community activities.

Accommodations should provide at least 40 square feet per child in the living areas. Classrooms and workshops should be spacious. Playground areas should be provided according to the number of children in the home. Toilets and bathrooms should have sufficient water supply and the number provided should also be according to the number of children. Diet should be well-balanced and nutritious. Basic and advanced education opportunities should be provided to all children. The truth, however, is that the children in these homes live in inhuman conditions far below the ideal outlined above.

The living areas are overcrowded, with the children often sleeping on the floors with just one dirty bed-sheet and usually without a pillow. They do not have proper clothing. Many of them do not even have undergarments. The food provided is not sufficient and often the younger children are bullied by the older ones to part with their food portion and thus go hungry. All the children stay hungry until late evening if there is a short supply of cooking gas. The homes offer no proper medical facilities.

Insufficient toilets and scarcity of water means they are not able to bathe regularly, which results in unhygienic personal habits and associated skin diseases and other ailments.

The facilities provide no emotional counseling or support.

They provide no moral education. These homes are cesspools of crime where the younger children learn anti-social behavior from the older ones. They breed all types of crime, from bootlegging and petty theft to more serious crimes like rape and murder.

The children have hardly any entertainment or fun times. They have to resort to their own means for having fun, often with disastrous consequences.

If they are fortunate, they get sent out to other NGOs where they receive much better care. If they are sent on to other government-run homes, however, their misery continues.

The sad part is that many of the children sent to these homes had never committed a crime before they came but leave the home as hardened criminals.

Due to rural poverty, family members—especially young people—migrate to Mumbai city in search of jobs and better living conditions and end up in overcrowded slum communities. Rural poverty and urban growth have thrust thousands of helpless children onto the streets, over-stretching the meager resources available in the city and exposing the children to disease, abuse and exploitation.

Most street children in Mumbai are forced to beg. They are usually young runaways who have left home for various reasons—especially because of poverty. Apart from these are the abandoned and destitute orphans and the children of prostituted women who have no place to stay. In addition, some parents hire out their children to beg on the streets.

They can be seen at almost all busy traffic signals, outside hotels of disrepute, at railway stations, etc. To most of the inhabitants of Mumbai, they are no more than a nuisance with no rights to dignity, love or care. In a country where human life is expendable, they die as they have lived: unwanted and unknown to the civilized world.

We, however, see the true plight of these children—they are made to stand on the roads in rainy cold weather or in the burning heat of the day with precious little clothing or protection. We have often seen the smaller ones killed or severely injured by speeding cars. Very often, some of the children are deliberately maimed (an arm or leg cut off or an eye gouged out) to make them seem more pitiable to passersby, prompting them to give alms. It is at this point that they are used by organized gangs or petty anti-social elements and get inducted into a life of crime. If they get caught, they are expendable and other children take their places. They are too young to disclose the name or location of the persons who recruited them and are therefore considered to be very convenient "employees"—all they want in return is a good meal or a cheap toy! The vicious cycle goes something like this:

Poverty ... streets ... petty crime ... remand

homes ... anti-social influences ... hardened criminals.

While we want to do everything in our power to help the children who are already in prison, we would rather pursue the path of prevention. Our main objective is to rescue children from the street *before* they are exploited and abused and evolve into hardened criminals. Establishing shelters for such children needs to be done as a top priority.

THE EARTHQUAKE

Doug and Ramona Jacobs have been on the frontlines of the fight against child exploitation in Nepal. Their work in Western Nepal, from where girls are smuggled into India, has been effective in closing the borders to traffickers. They have also been strong advocates of AIDS prevention.

After graduating from Auburn University, Doug enrolled at Southeastern University. That is where we first met Doug and Ramona. Impressed by their abilities and passion for the lost, we planted seeds in their hearts about one day working in Southern Asia. They were serving at an inner-city outreach in 1993 in Mobile, Alabama, when North India was hit by a catastrophic earthquake. As they watched news footage of the disaster, their burden for Southern Asia grew. We invited Doug to join us for a three-week visit to Nepal. Six months later, the Jacobses relocated to Nepal. They didn't come to Nepal to start Project Rescue, but they couldn't ignore the need. "When you sense that God's heart is breaking over this situation," Doug said, "and you enter into fellowship with His sufferings, you know you have to do something."

SISTER AMBIKA

Ambika Pandey was raised in a high caste family. After receiving Jesus as her Savior, she enrolled in Bible college. She married a young man who served as the pastor of a congregation in Kolkata, India. After receiving her master's degree in theology, Ambika took a position as a Bible college professor.

A burden for the women in prostitution in Kolkata and their children began to well up in her heart. For many years she had dreamed of reaching out to them, but because of her family's prominent standing she kept it to herself. When Sisters from Mother Teresa's order came to the Assemblies of God mission and asked for someone to take over the Bible classes for the children in the red-light district, Ambika quickly volunteered. Every week, for three years, she held a Bible study

in the red-light district. That was the start of
Project Rescue in Kolkata. A night-care program
for the children of the brothels was launched,
providing them with tutoring, food, clothing
and more. Later, vocational training was added,
which included prayer and daily devotions for the
women.

It is not unusual to see Ambika walking through
the maze known as the red-light district, praying
audibly for the girls to find Christ and freedom.
Despite the sight of known criminals crowding
around brothel stalls, she marches through the
narrow corridors as if nothing can harm her. She
knows she's on a mission from God.

MORE HOMES

After completing his university studies,
Mathew Daniel took a position on staff with
K.K. Devaraj at Bombay Teen Challenge. Gifted
in administration and under the mentorship
of Devaraj, he learned how to establish a
compassion ministry, develop a staff and work
with government laws regulating social work.
He felt a burden to expand the reach of Project
Rescue by establishing additional Homes of
Hope. Subsequently, he and his wife, Suhasini,
who earned her degree in social services, worked
closely with Doug and Ramona Jacobs to

open new Project Rescue sites for women in prostitution and their children in Nagpur, Pune and Chennai, India. They currently lead the Project Rescue Home of Hope in Pune, which is a pilot program to receive young women rescued by the government in brothel raids.

PRAYING FOR THE WORKERS

The toll on workers dealing with women and children who have experienced unimaginable acts of sexual perversion and violence is impossible to calculate. For those who offer care through the local church and Project Rescue, it is painful to listen to the victims' stories and difficult to comprehend how they have managed to survive. The emotional and physical wounds of sexual exploitation are deep, especially among children. Despite their theological and social training, some workers find it difficult to deal with the darkness and brutality day after day. They need the prayers of their brothers and sisters in Christ to sustain them. In 30 years of ministry, we have found ministry to victims of sexual trafficking and slavery to be the most challenging and spiritually intense that we have ever undertaken. Engaging in the battle against the most horrific forms of human depravity brings one face-to-face with the worst side of man without God and with the destructive power of Satan himself. But engaging in the battle against sexual slavery in the compassion of Christ and the power of His Spirit also brings one face-to-face with the life-changing power of God's grace in its truest form. We have seen how the love of Jesus shines most brightly in the darkest places.

THE LOCAL CHURCH

It is impossible to describe the scope and expansion of Project Rescue without discussing the vital role of the local church. Local churches in Southern Asia work in tandem with Project Rescue. In Bombay, for example, the Saturday church service is an entry point for prostituted women and their children. These women are nurtured in their newfound faith by members of the local church and encouraged to eventually enter a Home of Hope. The earlier victims and their daughters find Christ through the outreach of the red-light district church and BTC-Project Rescue, the better their chances are of not contracting AIDS. Churches in high-risk areas have also helped women in prostitution protect their daughters from becoming entrapped in the trade by helping them enter the Project Rescue childcare program.

As Project Rescue expands to other nations, it

will continue to work in concert with the local church. We are in the business of meeting physical and spiritual needs, but within the context of building the local church. Compassion ministry is not an end in itself; it is not a substitute for proclamation or discipleship. Both are part of the biblical mission as modeled by Jesus. That is why the local church is an integral part of Project Rescue.

Doors have opened in Moldova and Russia, from where women are being trafficked all over the world with false promises of a better life. Eventually, like Teen Challenge and its global approach to drug addiction, Project Rescue needs to respond to the worldwide sex-slave industry by forming a global network of cooperative ministries. It is our prayer that God will call more workers and churches to serve on the frontlines of this rescue effort.

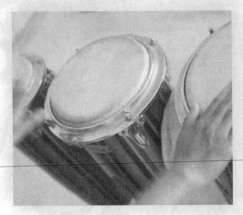

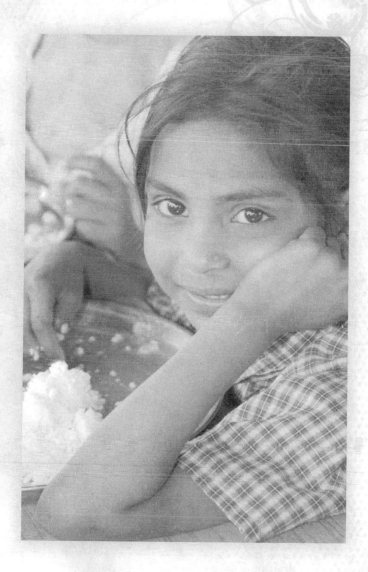

"At a certain point, I felt God is not looking for alms. God is looking for action."[1]

—*Bono*

CHAPTER ELEVEN

BEYOND SYMPATHY

Every day on his way to church in Kolkata, India, David passed large sewer pipes that were being inhabited by refugee families. One 5-year-old girl caught David's attention. Her face was smudged with dirt and her torn T-shirt was hanging off her shoulder. David smiled at her. She waved back and brushed her unkempt hair off her eyes. David noticed that she was alone with her 18-month-old brother. *Her parents must be away trying to find food,* David thought, on his way to an appointment.

The following day, when David walked by the pipes, the tiny girl ran and grabbed his pant leg.

"Hello!" he said with a chuckle.

She didn't respond. She merely rubbed her stomach and pointed to her little brother to signify they were hungry.

"You're hungry?" David asked, raising his fingers to his mouth to simulate eating.

Instantly she nodded her head, her listless eyes

pleading for help.

David had stared into countless faces of poverty. Fortunately he had not grown calloused to the pain and suffering. He knew Jesus was urging him to extend His compassion by feeding these precious children.

"Wait right here," he said. "Don't move. I'll bring you food."

He took off on a dead sprint to the church. He loaded enough rice and stew on a plate that it resembled a small volcano. He raced back to the pipes and handed the plate to the girl. Her eyes widened and a smile erupted on her face. "Thank you," she said in Bengali.

"You're welcome," David replied.

He watched as she carried the plate to safety inside their pipe-home, then took her brother by the hand and led him to the food. In amazement, David watched as she fed the tiny boy until he was full. Only then did she take a bite. Her brother's stomach was more important than her own.

Tears surfaced in David's eyes.

"God," he whispered to himself, "this little girl knows more about giving than almost any person I know—including me."

APATHY NOT AN OPTION

Millions of women and children are victims of the sex-slave industry. They are abused every day, with little hope of escape. The problem is monumental, the need overwhelming. In response to the crisis, some have chosen to throw up their hands and retreat. Others have chosen to ignore the problem altogether.

For followers of Jesus, apathy is not an option. Christians must respond to this human tragedy. But what can people do to help victims on the other side of the world?

First, we must realize that the human sex trade is not an evil confined to developing nations. It is a global tragedy. Its tentacles reach into virtually every nation and community. It has direct ties to pornography and organized crime. And the United States is one of the largest producers and purveyors of pornography in the world, which feeds this global appetite for sexual deviance. Economics—supply and demand—fuel the sex-slave industry. Thus, when we support decency standards in our own community or at the state and federal levels, we are helping young women escape the snares of these predators. We must let our voices be heard at our city councils and school boards. We need to speak out in the halls of our state capitols and in Washington, D.C. We must be a mouthpiece for the weak and abused in our courtrooms.

Second, we should devote ourselves to concerted prayer. The light and hope of the gospel will not pierce the darkness and liberate millions of women and girls without the prayer and determination of millions of believers. These words should be placed in every Bible owned by a follower of Jesus: "Dear Lord, please save the millions of women and girls who are being exploited in sexual slavery; and use my life and resources to save at least one." The rescue of innocent lives must become a priority. One way that we demonstrate our love for Jesus and our concern for these girls is to pray daily for their salvation and liberation.

Third, we must be willing to invest some of the resources God has entrusted to us. The enemy is investing billions of dollars to enslave young girls and women in prostitution. But God can take our $20 contribution, for example, and use it to snatch a life from the claws of the evil one.

Someone said that helping the poor and weak is "not about us; it's about them." Perhaps it should be said a different way: "It's about us ... them ... and Him." How we respond to the needs of the weak and exploited says a lot about our love for Christ and His creation. James 2:14-17 says, "What good is it, my brothers, if a man claims to have faith but has no deeds? Can such faith save him? Suppose a brother or sister is without clothes and daily food. If one of you says to him, 'Go, I wish you well; keep warm and well fed,' but does nothing about his physical needs, what good is it? In the same way, faith by itself, if it is not accompanied by action, is dead."

A contribution to ministries like Project Rescue will give hope and save lives. In turn, God promises to bless those who take up the cause of the weak. Psalm 41:1-3 says, "Blessed is he who has regard for the weak; the Lord delivers him in times of trouble. The Lord will protect him and preserve his life; he will bless him in the land and not surrender him to the desire of his foes. The Lord will sustain him on his sickbed and restore him from his bed of illness."

Many churches, organizations and individuals have answered the call to help rescue enslaved women and their children. Without their generosity, these women and children would have no hope. When the property for Ashagram became available, the congregation of First Assembly in North Little Rock, Arkansas, gave $100,000 to purchase the land. When the Women's Ministries of Southern California heard about Project Rescue, they established a "freedom fund." More than $400,000 was raised to care for the women and children that were coming out of the brothels. International Christian Assemblies of God Church in Hong Kong gave $100,000 to build Homes of

Hope. And many more individuals and churches have provided monthly financial support and given offerings so Project Rescue can save more lives.

Fourth, we can work for Christ to rescue victims by recruiting our friends and family members to get involved with ministries like Project Rescue—to move from the sidelines to the playing field. What could be accomplished if believers solicited the help and participation of their network of family and friends? Some have chosen to form home- work- and church-based cell groups for the cause of rescuing victims and taking a stand for decency and human rights. It has proven to be an effective way to share the love of Christ with neighbors who have an interest in fighting human exploitation.

Followers of Jesus also have a duty to rally support within their local church. It is easy for the victims of the sex-trafficking trade to get lost in the myriad of needs and missions opportunities that confront the local church. Each congregation needs at least one person who will take up the cause and speak on behalf of these victims. Each church, each person can do something to rescue another life from the dungeons of prostitution.

Fifth, some people are called to serve on the frontlines as rescue workers. Whether missions is a lifelong vocation or a short-term assignment, they feel compelled to go and serve. They want to dedicate their God-given talents to improving the lives of others. (See Appendix II, "A Statement from FAAST," what individuals can do to stop slavery and trafficking.)

More people can *give* than *go* to places like Bombay or Katmandu. But when people give, they are empowering Project Rescue workers to feed, clothe and provide shelter to young girls who have escaped the brothels. They are enabling Project Rescue to protect and educate the children of prostituted women. They are making it possible for Project Rescue workers to cradle and comfort the infants born with HIV. They are mobilizing church workers to go into the brothels and proclaim to women and girls that Jesus loves them.

The Psalmist reminds us that our cause of Project Rescue is a reflection of God's heart. He loves daughters and hates the evil that has devoured their hopes and stolen their dignity and self-worth. Psalm 72:12-14 says, "For he will deliver the needy who cry out, the afflicted who have no one to help. He will take pity on the weak and the needy and save the needy from death. He will rescue them from oppression and violence, for precious is their blood in his sight."

Someday, when we walk through the Pearly Gates, may God smile and nod approvingly at us because we did our part to take Christ's love *Beyond the Soiled Curtain.*

AFTERWORD

Beth was weary from the long journey to
Madras, India, but sleep would have to wait.
She felt a sense of urgency to speak to the young
women at the Project Rescue home. The girls had
planned a special program of music and dance in
her honor. And, in turn, she would bring them a
word of encouragement.

As she entered the room, the girls broke into
applause. Beth was ushered to a seat, and though
her eyes were heavy, she silently asked God to
deliver a timely and inspiring message through her.

The girls' musical presentation evoked tears
of joy in Beth's eyes; she was moved by their
expression of love and gratitude.

When it was Beth's turn to share, she quoted
Jeremiah 29:11: "'For I know the plans I have
for you,' declares the Lord, 'plans to prosper you
and not to harm you, plans to give you hope and
a future.'" "God has brought you to this place
because He loves you," she said. "You belong to
Him now. He is your Father. He created you. He
knows your future and your past. And, the future
He has for you is wonderful. Even when difficulty
comes your way, you can trust Him. He will take
care of you. Claim the promise of 1 Peter 5:7:

'Cast all your anxiety on him because he cares for you.'"

That night Beth prayed for the girls with whom she had shared. She knew that within 48 hours the young women and staff would face a major challenge. Just before arriving, she received news that they were being forced to vacate their rented Project Rescue facility in Madras. The landlord had received a higher offer and was essentially sending the girls away.

The girls and staff were deeply disturbed. They were losing the only safe place they had ever known.

The Project Rescue workers had encouraged them to pray: "God knows your future. When difficulty comes, pray to Him. He will help us. Jesus is with us!"

A similar situation arose at the Project Rescue home in Pune, India. The landlord simply said, "We want someone else using this property." His decision was undoubtedly influenced by the stigma associated with prostitution and its victims in India. Landlords believe it is "bad karma" to have "such women" living in their facilities.

Fortunately, in both Madras and Pune, God answered the prayers of the women, children and workers: facilities were found just in time.

The evictions in Madras and Pune were further evidence, however, that God desires permanence for those Project Rescue is trying to help. Owning facilities may not be essential in other parts of the world, but it is important in places like Southern Asia. It gives the women security and the ministry stability. When Project Rescue owns a building there is no landlord to strike fear in the hearts of these precious women and their children.

But Project Rescue is not about buildings. Facilities are merely a means of rebuilding and restoring lives. It is our prayer that individuals, churches, organizations and even businesses will join Project Rescue in declaring to the world, "Exploited women and children matter. We will give them a home. We will fight for their freedom. We will tell them that their Creator loves them and He has prepared a place for them in heaven where they will walk the streets of gold with their heads held high ... because they are children of a King."

A P P E N D I X I

PROJECT RESCUE AT A GLANCE— 1997 TO 2009

- 11 ministry-affiliated sites in 9 cities in India, Nepal and Moldova

- 11 Homes of Hope (aftercare homes for restoration–4 for women/girls rescued from prostitution, 4 for their daughters for prevention)

- 2 night-care centers for children of women in prostitution

- 7 vocational training centers

- 3 red-light district outreaches

- 3 red-light district churches

- 2 HIV/AIDS clinics

- 3 medical outreaches

- 6 awareness and prevention programs

- Approximately 4,500 exploited women and children ministered to

Project leader in development of *Hands That Heal: International Curriculum to Train Caregivers of Trafficking Survivors*, launched September 2007 on behalf of FAAST (Faith Alliance Against Slavery & Trafficking).

Projected ministry sites in the next five years:

- Bangalore, India

- Bangladesh (2010)

- Delhi, India (2010)

- Jaipur, India

- Russia

- Ukraine

MISSION STATEMENT

We exist to rescue and restore victims of sex trafficking through the love and power of Jesus Christ.

We believe that each child has been created by God with God-given purpose and the innate abilities to accomplish that purpose. We exist to help her discover that purpose and empower her to fulfill it.

We recognize the primary role of the local, national and global community of faith in the restoration process and are committed to empowering them to fulfill it.

We provide global awareness and opportunities for concerned partners to help bring freedom and a transformed future to those imprisoned in sexual slavery.

VALUE STATEMENT

The Project Rescue team upholds a framework of values to guide the daily actions of our leadership, staff and representatives. These values represent the standards that are used to measure our individual and collective actions.

A commitment to Christlike character.

> Project Rescue is committed to touching the
> exploited with the love of Jesus Christ. We
> endeavor to demonstrate His love in practical
> ways, providing food, a safe home, clothing,
> education, counseling, vocational training and
> medical care to rescued victims. We proclaim
> and endeavor to live God's unconditional love,
> His provision of forgiveness, and His pathway
> of acceptance open to all who are broken by
> sin.

A commitment to treating each person with
respect and dignity.

> Project Rescue values each individual as
> a person of eternal value with strengths,
> weaknesses, intelligence, emotions and dreams.
> We help them face the painful traumas of their
> past to find healing in a loving, supportive
> community of staff who are committed to
> their total restoration. The restorative process
> empowers survivors to face their future with
> health and hope in Jesus Christ.

A commitment to our partners and employees.

Project Rescue strives to work collaboratively
to achieve our goals. We are committed to
a ministry environment characterized by
continuous learning, passionate faith, and
a team orientation. We seek to work with
the best-qualified people in the process of
restoring victims in order to conduct our
mission with professionalism and integrity. All
resources entrusted to us are valued as a gift
from God to be used effectively, responsibly
and accountably in bringing new life to
exploited women and girls.

APPENDIX II

A STATEMENT FROM FAAST

Project Rescue is a member of the Faith Alliance Against Slavery and Trafficking (FAAST), based in Alexandria, Virginia. Following is a statement from that consortium:

The mission of FAAST is to eliminate human trafficking through prevention, prosecution, victim protection, and sustainable restoration. Our target population includes all those victimized by human trafficking: children and adults, males and females.

FAAST engages in the following types of interventions:

1. Prevention: education for communities, faith-based groups and vulnerable populations; advocacy, and demand reduction initiatives.

2. Prosecution: legal advocacy, legal education, and training for law enforcement and the judiciary.

3. Victim Identification and Protection: training for staff and affiliates worldwide, victim identification and protection, safe communication and networks for people at risk, and holistic mental and physical health assessments and services.

4. Sustainable Restoration: educational and vocational training, holistic reintegration, and micro-enterprise development.

FAAST unites the resources and efforts of individual members to strengthen their responses to the scourge of human trafficking in its various manifestations including slave labor, domestic servitude, sexual servitude, begging, forced combat, and illicit removal of body parts. FAAST's approach is rooted in the ability of faith-based organizations to reach into troubled regions where government and non-governmental organizations are unable to sustain their presence. Despite war, famine, and socioeconomic and political breakdowns, the church structure, through which the Alliance works, often remains intact.

Trafficking in persons (TIP) is a global human rights tragedy and criminal activity. The combination of poverty, unemployment, gender inequality (especially the low status of girl children), inadequate legislation, and poor law

enforcement all enable TIP to thrive. The Faith
Alliance Against Slavery and Trafficking (FAAST)
has been working with government ministries as
well as community leaders to help them understand
the definition and significance of TIP. While
significant gains have been made to raise awareness
and reduce trafficking, much remains undone.

The direct care of trafficking victims is complex
and organizations are responding to aspects of this
need with safe houses, counseling, limited training
for caregivers, and other interventions. However,
a comprehensive curriculum developed by FAAST
guides the caregiver in how to effectively and
appropriately respond to the complex needs of
the trafficked person. This curriculum coincides
with a statement from the U.S. Department of
State, Global Trafficking in Persons Office: "In
addressing the link between human trafficking and
HIV/AIDS, it is clear that we will need to step up
preventative programs, for only when we prevent
trafficking, and prevent the spread of the HIV/
AIDS epidemic, will we truly be successful."

According to the U.S. State Department, an
estimated 42 million people live with HIV/AIDS
worldwide. While the global epidemic of HIV/
AIDS affects various populations, women and
children who are trafficked for prostitution and
other sexual purposes are particularly impacted.

Due to the violent nature of sex with trafficked victims, the lack of control over the circumstances and number of "customers," the inability to insist on regular condom use, and the youth of many trafficked victims, victims of sex trafficking are severely at risk for contracting HIV. The public health implications of sex trafficking extend beyond its victims to those who frequent brothels and who can become carriers and/or core transmitters of serious diseases, to the general public. Some experts have linked sex trafficking to the spread and mutation of the AIDS virus, suggesting that sex trafficking facilitates the global dispersion of HIV subtypes.

While the link between HIV and TIP has been noted, few organizations are taking practical steps to overlap related programs. FAAST targets populations affected by both issues (e.g., women/girls, refugees, people involved in high-risk sexual activity, destitute persons) with assistance information, and conducts TIP education and training for service providers working with persons vulnerable to or affected by HIV/AIDS. Because FAAST members are networked in over 200 countries around the world, we are able to implement successful referral, educational and awareness projects efficiently and effectively through our faith communities in Africa, Asia, the Americas and Europe.

APPENDIX III

WHAT INDIVIDUALS CAN DO TO STOP SLAVERY AND TRAFFICKING

Be a 21st-century abolitionist. Get involved in the fight to stop modern-day slavery and trafficking in your neighborhood and around the world. This list is a starting point for action.

PRAY

Commit yourself to regular prayer for trafficking issues in the United States and around the world.

Organize your Sunday school class, Bible study, or another group to pray regularly.

Please pray for every person that is currently a victim enslaved today that they will be freed from their captivity. Also, pray for trafficking survivors that they will be made whole again, physically, spiritually and emotionally. Pray for their continued safety and possible reintegration back into their families and communities.

Pray for FAAST personnel who work tirelessly at the front lines of the fight against trafficking. They protect and care for victims, educate communities and government members about trafficking, and work to enforce laws against traffickers. They work in dangerous situations every day, putting themselves in harm's way to protect the vulnerable. Please pray for their spiritual, psychological, and physical strength and safety.

Pray that national leaders will rise up against slavery and trafficking in countries supplying and countries demanding victims of trafficking.

Pray for the children, women and men in FAAST partner projects and communities who are vulnerable to trafficking because of their poverty and lack of opportunities.

Pray for traffickers and other facilitators of trafficking, that they would be convicted, repent, and stop their callous behavior.

LEARN

Learn about trafficking and modern-day slavery. Visit the FAAST Web site at www.faastinternational.org.

Download or request the latest Trafficking in Persons Report from the U.S. Department of State Office to Monitor and Combat Trafficking. Go to www.state.gov/g/tip/rls/tiprpt/2009 or call 1(202) 312-9639.

Sign up for the latest news and information about sexual trafficking from the Initiative Against Sexual Trafficking (IAST) at www.iast.net; other forms of human trafficking at www.humantrafficking.org.

Find out what's happening in your state. Sign up for the U.S. Policy Alert Service through the Polaris Project at www.polarisproject.org and receive regular updates, maps, and alerts on legislative developments on trafficking in the United States.

Go on a study tour with a FAAST partner organization.

READ

Disposable People, Kevin Bales

Understanding Global Slavery, Kevin Bales

Enslaved: True Stories of Modern Day Slavery,
    edited by Jesse Sage and Liora Kasten

Prostitution, Trafficking and Traumatic Stress,
    Melissa Farley

*Commercial Sexual Exploitation of Children:
    Youth Involved in Prostitution, Pornography
    & Sex Trafficking*, Laura A. Barnitz

The Natashas: Inside the New Global Sex Trade,
    Victor Malerek

Human Traffic: Sex, Slaves & Immigration, Craig
    McGill

Slavery: A World History, Milton Metzler

Sold, Patricia McCormick

*Sex Trafficking: The Global Market in Women
    and Children*, Kathryn Farr

Not for Sale, Kevin Batsone

WATCH

Born into Brothels: Calcutta's Red Light Kids (2005)

Fields of Mudan, a 23-minute film about child sex
   slavery in Asia (2004)

Human Trafficking, the 4-hour Lifetime miniseries
   on European women trafficked into the U.S.A.
   for prostitution (2005)

Amazing Grace, the inspiring true story of
   William Wilberforce who demanded abolition
   of the African slave trade in the U.K. in the
   1800s (2007)

Modern-Day Slavery: Sierra Leone and Liberia,
   a 10-minute video by FAAST partners World
   Hope and World Relief on trafficking and our
   programs in these countries (2006)

Trade, Sex trade into the United States (2007)

Holly, a 1 hour 54 min. movie on child trafficking
   in Cambodia (2007)

Very Young Girls, a documentary that follows several
   New York city tween and teenagers who are
   domestically trafficked and are trying to cope with
   the consequences and redirect their lives (2008)

EDUCATE

Talk about human trafficking. Tell your friends, share with your pastor, inform your family.

Host an anti-trafficking event or presentation on slavery and trafficking at your church, school, Bible study, or other community forum. Contact FAAST for speaker suggestions and availability.

Hang an anti-trafficking poster in your church, business, or office. Posters advertising the U.S. Department of Health and Human Services (HHS) victim hotline are a valuable outreach tool to potential victims and those who may come into contact with victims. Sample posters are available at www.acf.hhs.gov/trafficking/index.html or (888) 373-7888. Posters are available in English, Spanish, Thai, Vietnamese, Indonesian, Chinese, and Korean.

Provide anti-trafficking materials (books, pamphlets, flyers, dvds) at informational tables or booths. Materials are available from FAAST or HHS.

Post signs, posters and other help information in public places. Advertisements in train stations, airports, buses, libraries, rest stops, and gas stations with hotline and help information in

multiple languages will help victims find their way
to safety.

Preach a sermon about slavery, what the Bible
says about it, the urgency to abolish slavery and
trafficking, and the need to reaffirm the inherent,
God-given dignity of human beings. Contact
FAAST for a list of Bible references to slavery.

Introduce a book or movie on slavery and
trafficking into your book club, Sunday school, or
other gathering.

Write articles and/or letters of opinion for
local papers, church, denominational, or other
publications.

Speak on a form of slavery (sex, labor, servitude,
etc.) in a class at your local middle school, high
school or college. Educating youth and young
adults on these topics will not only curb demand
through education, but will also raise up future
abolitionists.

ADVOCATE

Ask your state legislators what they've done
to stop sex trafficking and labor trafficking in
your state. If they don't know, offer to provide

information on what they can do. For more information, see the U.S. Department of Justice webpage on slavery and trafficking at www.usdoj.gov/crt/crim/tpwetf.htm, and the model state law on trafficking at www.usdoj.gov/crt/crim/model_state_law.pdf.

Find out if your state has an Anti-Trafficking Task Force. If not, suggest that one be formed. If so, find out how you can help. More information on state action is available at www.polarisproject.org.

Provide information to your legislators on how demand increases supply in your state. For more information, contact FAAST. For information on how the sex industry (strip clubs, prostitution rings, pornography) increases demand for victims in your state, contact the Initiative Against Sexual Trafficking (IAST) at www.iast.net or call (703) 159-5896.

Teach youth and young adults about the link between the sex industry and the sex trade. Stop the demand before it starts. Order the six-session curriculum for youth in grades 7, 8, and 9 from Adults Saving Kids and organize a viewing with church youth groups, scouts, etc. It creates awareness of the dangers of commercial sexual exploitation. Contact ahartman@adultssavingkids. org or call (612) 872-0684.

SERVE

Contact FAAST for current volunteer opportunities in the U.S. or abroad. FAAST welcomes volunteers to do research, writing, graphic design, law review, organize events, staff information booths at events, and more.

Organize an anti-trafficking group in your school or church committed to getting educated, educating others, and supporting organizations that work on trafficking issues.

Host an evening at your home to show your friends one of the films listed above. Talk about how the issue of human trafficking impacts you. Provide this list for further action.

Create and distribute T-shirts or stickers with anti-trafficking slogans.

Work with existing social service agencies to help survivors of trafficking. Survivors are often in desperate need of food, clothing, shelter, translators, medical attention, transportation, crisis counseling and other services.

Represent a client. Many victims of trafficking in the U.S. need pro bono legal services to be certified as a victim of trafficking and apply for T-

visas. Contact social service agencies in your area
to see how you can help.

Collect items for care packages for survivors.
Collaborate with existing service providers to
find out what they need. Based on cultural and
climate conditions, the types of goods collected for
care packages may vary, so be sure to discuss with
program directors before sending items.

Combat demand for victims of sex trafficking.
Work in your community to seek the arrest of
buyers of commercial sex, develop deterrent sex-
offender programs, encourage victim-centered law
enforcement to punish perpetrators and protect
victims.

REPORT

Learn how to identify victims of trafficking. **Look**
for signs of trafficking. **Listen** for indications
of trafficking. Victims are often hidden in plain
view.

If you have information or suspect that slavery or
trafficking is happening near you, **report** it to the
U.S. Department of Health and Human Services
Trafficking Information and Referral Hotline at
(888) 373-7888, or the U.S. Department of Justice

Trafficking in Persons Complaint Line at (888)
428-7581, or contact the FBI field office nearest
you. Your call could save lives.

GIVE

Demand "slave-free" goods. Buy rugs carrying
the Rugmark symbol; fair trade coffee, tea and
cocoa; shop at "fair trade" stores such as Ten
Thousand Villages; look for the Fairtrade label
(see www.fairtrade.net); ask stores to stock fairly
traded items.

Ask hard questions about your investments.
Are you assured that your investments are not
linked to slave labor? If not, move your money
to an ethical fund that does not profit from
slave labor. Visit researching ethical investment
companies at the Open Directory Project at http://
dmoz.org/Business/Investing/Socially_Responsible/
Financial_and_Investment_Advisors.

Ask your church missions directors if they
are supporting anti-trafficking programs or
organizations. If not, encourage resources to be
used for anti-trafficking efforts.

Encourage your church or other gathering place to
buy fair-trade coffee instead of cheaper coffee of

unknown origin for their fellowship time. Learn about church-based coffee campaigns at http:// new.gbgm-umc.org/umcor/work/hunger/fair-trade/ coffee/?search=coffee.

Donate. The U.S. gave over $260 billion to charities in 2006 (75% from individual donors), but less than 2.5% of those funds were designated for international development, including overseas anti-trafficking efforts.

Used by permission of FAAST.

ENDNOTES

Statistics
1. U.S. Department of State, Office to Monitor and Combat Trafficking in Persons, "Trafficking in Persons Report: 2008."
2. U.S. Department of State, "2008 Human Rights Report: India" (February 25, 2009), www.state.gov.
3. UNICEF, "Child Protection Information Sheet: Commercial Sexual Exploitation" (2006), http://www.unicef.org/protection/files/Sexual_Exploitation.pdf.
4. Bureau of Democracy, Human Rights and Labor, "Human Rights Practices-India" (March 8, 2006).
5. U.S. Department of State, "Other Bilateral Economic Assistance" (2006), http://www.state.gov/documents/organization/60645.pdf.

Chapter 1
1. www.quotationspage.com.

Chapter 2
1. "President Announces Initiatives to Combat Human Trafficking," http://georgewbush-whitehouse.archives.gov/news/releases/2004/07/20040716-11.html.
2. Amy Carmichael, *Life Principles*, InTouch Ministries.
3. Shelly Ngo with Sanjay Sojwal, "Sleeping With the Goddess" (World Outreach Ministries), http://www.houseofrefuge-india.org/sleeping_goddess.html.
4. Ibid.
5. Ibid.

Chapter 3
1. Vital Voices Global Partnership and NYU's Center for Global Affairs Public Forum (March 6, 2005).
2. U.S. Department of State, Office to Monitor and Combat Trafficking in Persons, "Trafficking in Persons Report: 2008."
3. U.S. Department of State, "Other Bilateral Economic Assistance" (2006), http://www.state.gov/documents/organization/60645.pdf.
4. Kevin Bales, *Disposable People: New Slavery in the Global Economy* (Los Angeles: University of California Press, 1999).
5. Kent Hill presentation to Consortium of faith-based initiatives on human trafficking (Washington, D.C., 2005).
6. Victor Malarek, *The Natashas: Inside the New Global Sex Trade* (New York: Arcade Publishing, 2003).
7. Bales, op. cit.

Chapter 4
1. Colin L. Powell, letter in "Trafficking in Persons Report," U.S. Department of State, Office to Monitor and Combat Trafficking in Persons, June 11, 2003.
2. David Helcher, "Child Sex Tourism," p. 3.
3. Sergeant Marcus Frank, *Asian Criminal Enterprises and Prostitution* (Special Investigations Unit Intelligence/Organized Crime, Westminster, Calif. Police Department). From an edited version of a paper presented at the 24th International Asian Organized Crime Conference held in Chicago, Illinois (March 25-29, 2002).

Chapter 5
1. www.quotationspage.com.
2. Swapna Majumdar, "Preteens in Indian Caste Forced Into Prostitution," *Women's enews* (April 2002), http://www.womensenews.org/story/the-world/020429/preteens-indian-caste-forced-prostitution.

Chapter 6
1. www.state.gov/secretary.
2. Holly Burkhalter, U.S. Policy Director of Physicians for Human Rights, in *Trafficking in Persons: A Global Review; Hearing Before the Subcommittee on International Terrorism, Nonproliferation and Human Rights of the Committee on International Relations, House of Representatives. One Hundred Eighth Congress, Second Session, June 24, 2004, http://commdocs.house.gov/committees/intlrel/hfa94512.000/hfa94512_0.htm#FR5.
3. Ibid.
4. Amy Waldman, "On India's Roads, Cargo and a Deadly Passenger" (December 6, 2005), http://www.nytimes.com/2005/12/06/international/asia/06highway.html?ex=1291525200&en=d9e7bebfb6a59 24d&ei=5088&partner=rssnyt&emc=rss.
5. "India's AIDS Children Shunned (Human Rights Group: Infected Kids Discriminated In Education, Healthcare)", http://www.cbsnews.com/stories/2004/07/28/world/main632654.shtml.
6. Ibid.
7. UNAIDS, the Joint United Nations Programme on HIV/AIDS, "Report on the Global AIDS Epidemic" (2006), p. 82.
8. Ibid, p. 81.
9. Ibid, p. 106.

Chapter 7
1. www.brainyquote.com.
2. Michael Horowitz, "How to Win Friends and Influence Culture," *Christianity Today* (September 2005).

Chapter 8
1. Remarks to Secretary's Open Forum (Washington, D.C., May 25, 2004), www.state.gov.

Chapter 9
1. www.quotationspage.com.

Chapter 10
1. www.stanford.edu/group/King.

Chapter 11
1. www.quotationspage.com.

ABOUT THE AUTHORS

David and Beth Grant have served, along with K.K. Devaraj, as the founders and visionaries of Project Rescue. Their passion to share their faith and see sex-trafficking victims rescued and restored has carried them to more than 30 countries around the world. Together they serve on the Faith Alliance Against Slavery and Trafficking (FAAST), based in Alexandria, Virginia. For more than 30 years David and Beth have served in India.

In his early days in India, David served alongside Mark and Huldah Buntain in Calcutta. David is a widely sought after speaker and lecturer, and the recipient of numerous honors and awards. Millions of dollars have been raised to fund compassion and educational projects around the world through his efforts.

Beth earned her Ph.D. in intercultural education from Biola University and her M.A. in cultural anthropology from Assemblies of God Theological Seminary, where she currently serves on the board of directors. A renowned speaker and lecturer, she has coordinated national conferences for women in ministry, inspiring them to fulfill God's purposes for their lives.

David and Beth have two daughters, Rebecca and Jennifer, who share their parents' passion for rescuing the victims of sexual slavery.

AN OPPORTUNIT

❑ YES, I want to help rescue young women and children from sexual slavery.

❑ $30 per month will provide night-care shelter for a child whose mother is in the red-light district.

❑ $100 per month will provide care for a rescued victim living in a Home of Hope.

❑ $1,000 per month will cover operational expenses for a Home of Hope.

❑ $90,000 will help provide a Home of Hope.

Name _____

Address_____

City/State/Zip _____

Phone _____

E-mail Address _____

PROJECT RESCUE
P.O. Box 922 / Springfield, MO 65801 / 417-833-5564
www.projectrescue.com

Donations: Project Rescue, AGWM Acct. #6149520 (44)
All contributions are tax-deductible as allowed by law.

MAKE A DIFFERENCE

FOR MORE INFORMATION

Contact:

Project Rescue
P.O. Box 922
Springfield, MO 65801

417-833-5564

projectrescue@projectrescue.com
www.projectrescue.com

For more books offered by Onward Books:

www.onwardbooks.com

Onward Books, Inc.
4848 S. Landon Ct.
Springfield, MO 65810
417-425-4674